CANADA YEAR BY YEAR

Written by Elizabeth MacLeod

Illustrated by Sydney Smith

Kids Can Press

To Elaine Welden, a great Canadian and loving mother,
dedicated on behalf of Barbara Morgan — E.M.

For all the children of Canada — S.S.

Acknowledgements

Thank you to the authors of The Kids Book Of series who allowed their writing
to appear in this book: Jane Drake, Barbara Greenwood, Carlotta Hacker, Pat Hancock,
Ann Love, Briony Penn, the late Diane Silvey and Valerie Wyatt. I really appreciate your contributions.

Many thanks to Sydney Smith for his fabulous illustrations that truly make Canadian history come alive.

Organizing the many elements of this book was incredibly involved, and editor Katie Scott
did a great job. I also really appreciated her suggestions and comments throughout the process.
Designer Julia Naimska brought her wonderful and creative skills to the difficult task of
combining together all the illustrations and text components. Thank you as ever!

I'm very grateful to copy editor Catherine Dorton, fact checker Olga Kidisevic and production editor
DoEun Kwon for reading the text so carefully and correcting any errors. Thank you also to expert reviewer
Dr. Dean F. Oliver, director of research, Canadian Museum of History, as well as the whole team at Kids Can Press.

I'm always grateful for the support of my dad, as well as my brothers, Douglas and John.
And special thanks to Paul, a great Canadian who puts up with me year by year!

This book contains excerpts from *The Kids Book of Aboriginal Peoples in Canada, The Kids Book of Canada, The Kids Book of Canada at War, The Kids Book of the Far North, The Kids Book of Canadian Firsts, The Kids Book of Canadian Geography, The Kids Book of Canadian History, The Kids Book of Canadian Prime Ministers, The Kids Book of Great Canadians* and *The Kids Book of Great Canadian Women.* We are grateful to the authors of these books for permission to reproduce their material.

Kids Can Press gratefully acknowledges the financial support of the Government of Ontario, through the Ontario Media Development Corporation; the Ontario Arts Council; the Canada Council for the Arts; and the Government of Canada, through the CBF, for our publishing activity.

The Canadian flag is reproduced with the kind permission of the Department of Canadian Heritage.
The Canadarm is rendered with approval from the Canadian Space Agency.

The excerpt from the Declaration of Kinship and Cooperation is printed with the kind permission of the Assembly of First Nations.

Published in Canada and the U.S. by Kids Can Press Ltd.
25 Dockside Drive, Toronto, ON M5A 0B5

Kids Can Press is a Corus Entertainment Inc. company

www.kidscanpress.com

Edited by Katie Scott
Designed by Julia Naimska

Printed and bound in Shenzhen, China, in 3/2017 by C & C Offset

CM 16 0 9 8 7 6 5 4 3

Library and Archives Canada Cataloguing in Publication

MacLeod, Elizabeth, author
      Canada year by year / written by Elizabeth MacLeod ; illustrated by Sydney Smith.

ISBN 978-1-77138-397-4 (bound)

      1. Canada — History — Juvenile literature. I. Smith, Sydney, 1980–, illustrator II. Title.

FC172.M35 2016   j971   C2015-907041-4

CONTENTS

A COUNTRY IS BORN

At the stroke of midnight on July 1, 1867, Canadians began to celebrate the birth of their new country. Guns boomed, bells chimed and people cheered. A huge bonfire was lit in Ottawa, the new capital. Even though it was the middle of the night, people poured into the streets.

That afternoon, parades led by brass bands proudly marched down the main streets of many cities and towns. The sun shone brightly in each of the founding provinces. It was a perfect day to celebrate. At night, fireworks lit up the sky before happy Canadians wearily headed home after such an important day. For the first time, they had a strong feeling of unity as their nation took its place in the world. They looked forward to a promising future, full of growth and prosperity.

Although Canada didn't become a country until 1867, it already had a long history. The Vikings were the first explorers to arrive from Europe. When they sailed to what's now Newfoundland around the year 1000, they were met by Aboriginal peoples, who had been living on the land for thousands of years. The name Canada actually comes from the Huron-Iroquois word *kanata*, which means "village." Around 1535, French explorer Jacques Cartier began using the name to describe parts of the country.

Aboriginal peoples knew how to survive the cold, difficult climate. Some of these groups had learned how to plant crops and care for them so they would provide lots of food. When Europeans built permanent settlements in the 1600s, Aboriginal peoples taught them how to hunt and fish. They also knew what plants provided medicine. Their knowledge saved the lives of many explorers and settlers.

Throughout its long history, Canada has been a place where people have come to make their homes. Before becoming its own country, it was part of the French colonies called New France, and later part of the British colonies of British North America. Even today, about 250 000 newcomers arrive in Canada each year, bringing skills that help make the country a better place to live.

Canada's history is the story of its people and their inventions, discoveries and happenings that changed the world and how we live. This book is a year-by-year look at this history, from 1867 to 2017. All of the events in the country's history would never fit into one book, but many important ones are here.

These events — both good and bad — have transformed the lives of Canadians. The country's people will continue to shape not only Canada, but also the world.

What a Country!

Canada is a big place. In fact, it's the second-largest country in the world. It holds about 10 percent of the entire world's forests. And some of its parks are bigger than entire countries!

Canada also has the longest coastline in the world by far, and no bay on Earth has as long a shoreline as Hudson Bay. You'll find thousands of lakes in Canada — more than the rest of the world combined. That's definitely something to celebrate!

A NEW COUNTRY 1867–1884

In 1867, Canada became a new country — a confederation of just four provinces. Canadians were full of hope and excitement as they saw their nation growing.

Most Canadians were farmers in the mid-1800s. In rural areas, forestry was an important industry, and mining was increasing. In many cities, people went to work in factories and workshops as manufacturing developed.

Canadian streets looked very different in the 1860s. There were no cars. Street lights and office buildings were lit by gas lamps, not by electricity like today. In homes, people still burned candles or oil lamps for light and cooked on wood-burning stoves.

By the 1860s, technology was changing daily life. Railways connected more and more towns. Journeys that once took days by horse and carriage now could be done in hours. Mail also was transported faster by rail. An underwater telegraph cable had been laid across the Atlantic Ocean from Newfoundland to Ireland. Now, Canada could quickly get news from Europe.

1867 Confederation

By the 1860s, the colonies in what is now Canada knew it was time for change. There was fear that the United States would take them over, and Britain no longer wanted to pay to defend them. As well, the colonies weren't growing as quickly as they might because it was difficult for them to sell goods to one another — transportation between them was extremely poor. They began to think of banding together to become stronger and more successful.

It took three conferences, lots of debate and almost three years, but finally on July 1, 1867, the new country of Canada was created. It consisted of the provinces of New Brunswick, Nova Scotia, Ontario (formerly Canada West) and Quebec (formerly Canada East). Confederation, or the union of provinces into a new country, depended on the vision and determination of the Fathers of Confederation, many of whom dreamed of a powerful new nation that would eventually stretch from the Atlantic Ocean to the Pacific Ocean.

Most Famous Fathers of Confederation

George Brown acted for Canada West in the Confederation talks. An excellent speaker, he was one of the first people to suggest uniting the colonies. Before becoming a politician, he founded Toronto's *Globe* newspaper, which later became the *Globe and Mail* (page 48).

Georges-Étienne Cartier was a French-Canadian leader who was very supportive of Confederation. He played an important role in persuading the French of Canada East to join the nation. With Sir John A. Macdonald, he was co-premier of Canada East and Canada West from 1857 to 1862.

Alexander Galt represented English speakers in Canada East. He was a brilliant businessperson and was strongly in favour of Confederation. He wanted a railway across the country and knew Confederation would make it easier to build one.

Thomas D'Arcy McGee was known as the best public speaker of his time. He felt that Canada was a better place to live than the United States, so he supported Confederation to prevent the United States from taking over the colonies. He was one of the few politicians ever assassinated in Canada.

Samuel L. Tilley was a businessperson before he became a politician. He believed that Confederation could help the colonies prosper. As premier of New Brunswick, he also wanted a railway to connect the Maritimes to the other colonies.

Charles Tupper attended the Confederation meetings as premier of Nova Scotia and was greatly in favour of the union. In 1896, he became Canada's shortest-serving prime minister. When he died, he was the last survivor of the 36 Fathers of Confederation.

PROFILE

Sir John A. Macdonald

Sir John A. Macdonald from Canada West was a leading Father of Confederation. He played such a large part in Confederation that he was made Canada's first prime minister on July 1, 1867. He added three more provinces and a territory to Canada and began building a transcontinental railway (page 14) to span the nation and connect the provinces.

"*Whatever you do, adhere to the union. We are a great country, and shall become one of the greatest in the universe if we preserve it.*"

— Sir John A. Macdonald

When Did They Join Canada?

1867	New Brunswick, Nova Scotia, Ontario, Quebec
1870	Manitoba, Northwest Territories
1871	British Columbia
1873	Prince Edward Island
1898	Yukon Territory
1905	Alberta, Saskatchewan
1949	Newfoundland (later Newfoundland and Labrador)
1999	Nunavut

1868 The military expands

In its early days, Canada didn't have a trained army. Instead, it had a militia — ordinary citizens who volunteered to fight. They fought alongside professional soldiers, called regulars, from France or Britain. When British troops stationed in Canada left during the 1850s to fight in the Crimean War, a permanent Canadian militia was set up.

In 1868, the Militia Act was passed to give the new country control over its military. It also grew the active militia to 40 000 volunteers and created a reserve militia of men between the ages of 18 and 60 who could be called into action if needed.

By the late 1800s, Canada established regiments of professional soldiers. Their main job was training militia units, but they also fought during the Red River Rebellion (pages 18–19) and the South African War (pages 26–27) alongside militia volunteers.

Both part-time and regular forces in Canada were known as militia until World War II. In the 1950s, the militia became the Reserve Force. Today, this part-time group still supports units from the Canadian Armed Forces, which was formed on February 1, 1968, when the Canadian Army, Royal Canadian Navy and Royal Canadian Air Force merged.

1869 Photos in print

Until a photograph of Prince Arthur was published in the *Canadian Illustrated News* on October 30, 1869, books, magazines and newspapers used drawings to accompany their stories. An engraver named William Leggo and the Montreal publisher he worked for, Georges-Édouard Desbarats, figured out how to break down a photo into tiny dots that, when printed, would fool the eye into seeing a picture. The *Canadian Illustrated News* would become the first newspaper to consistently publish photographs of this quality — not just in Canada, but worldwide!

1870 Fenian raids

In the 1860s and 1870s, Canadians were being threatened by Fenian raids. Fenians were Irish Americans who wanted to end British rule in Ireland. They hoped that by capturing Canada as a hostage, they could convince Britain to grant Ireland independence.

Fenians attacked New Brunswick in April 1866, Ontario two months later and Quebec in 1870. They had planned to raid Manitoba in 1871 but were stopped at the American border.

Although the Fenians were never a major threat, they frightened people. The early raids had been one of the events that convinced Canadians they should unite as one country in 1867.

1871 Irish immigration

Beginning in the late 1840s, a large number of people came to Canada from Ireland. Many of them were escaping Ireland's potato famine. When the first Dominion of Canada census was taken in 1871, almost one-quarter of the country's population were Irish. That made them the single largest ethnic group in English Canada.

Irish immigrants were also the biggest ethnic group in most of Canada's cities except Montreal and Quebec City. They were especially important in the construction of Ontario's Rideau Canal and Quebec's Lachine Canal.

Angus McKay

In 1871, Angus McKay became the first Aboriginal person elected to Canada's government. Angus was the Member of Parliament (a politician elected by the people to the House of Commons) for Marquette, Manitoba, just northwest of Winnipeg. He was Métis, which meant his background was both European and First Nations. However, he opposed the views of Métis leader Louis Riel (pages 18–19). Before becoming a Member of Parliament, Angus had been elected to Manitoba's first Legislative Assembly in 1870, and he was elected again to this provincial government in 1874.

1872 British home children

Between 1869 and the 1930s, about 100 000 children were brought to Canada from Great Britain. Some came from orphanages, also called "homes," so these newcomers were called "home children." Others came from parents who could no longer provide for their families. Dr. Thomas John Barnardo, a missionary dedicated to helping homeless children, sent about 30 000 orphaned children from Britain to Canada as early as 1872.

The children had to work in homes or on farms in Canada, mostly in small towns and rural areas. They were supposed to be given allowances, clothes, meals and the chance to go to school. Instead, many had difficult lives. Some sisters and brothers were separated, while other home children were treated like slaves and even beaten.

Today, more than 1 in 10 Canadians are related to home children. British Home Child Day is celebrated every year on September 28 in Ontario. Canada designated 2010 the Year of the British Home Child to honour their contributions to their adopted country.

1873 North-West Mounted Police

In the 1870s, the Prairies were becoming lawless and dangerous. So in 1873, the Canadian government created a central police force, the North-West Mounted Police. In 1920, the force became known as the Royal Canadian Mounted Police (RCMP). By 1974, women were allowed to join the RCMP, which today remains Canada's national police force.

1874 Bell's telephone breakthrough

Sound and speech were always on Alexander Graham Bell's mind. His mother was deaf, and his father was an elocutionist who taught people how to speak clearly. By 1870, both of his brothers had died of lung disease, so his parents decided to move from Scotland to where the air was clean — Canada. In 1871, "Aleck" (as he was known to friends and family) began teaching at a school for deaf people in Boston, Massachusetts. He was a patient and inventive teacher.

At night, Aleck experimented with sound. He wanted to improve the telegraph, an instrument that sent and received electric pulses over wires. In 1874, he had a breakthrough while visiting his parents in Brantford, Ontario. Aleck realized that with a few changes to the telegraph, he could pick up all the sounds of the human voice. The sounds moved thin metal discs, and these discs could change electric currents, allowing voices to be sent and received over wires.

However, knowing how to do something and actually doing it are very different things, Aleck found. Almost two years later in Boston, on March 10, 1876, Aleck was in one room tinkering with a transmitter, while his assistant, Thomas Watson, had a receiver connected by wire in another room. When Aleck accidentally spilled some acid, he shouted into his transmitter, "Mr. Watson, come here. I want to see you!"

Thomas came running into the room — he'd heard Aleck's voice over the receiver. The telephone was born. In a few months, Aleck also figured out how to send telephone messages long distance, between Brantford and Paris, Ontario.

Aleck went on to invent many things, from iceberg detectors to airplanes that set flight records (page 31). Some of the planes used in World War I were based on his designs. But he often said he preferred to be known as someone who had helped deaf people communicate.

> "An inventor can no more help inventing than he can help thinking or breathing."
>
> — Alexander Graham Bell

PROFILE

Henry Woodward

In the mid-1800s, inventors around the world were working to create a light bulb that would burn long enough to be useful. Those inventors included Toronto medical student Henry Woodward and hotel owner Matthew Evans.

Henry and Matthew succeeded and in 1874 received a patent (the right to use or sell an invention) for their creation. Unfortunately, they couldn't afford to develop their invention. They sold their patent to an American, Thomas Edison, who would become famous for his own light-bulb invention.

1875 Indoor hockey

The first organized game of indoor hockey was played on March 3, 1875, in Montreal after a group of McGill University students made a list of rules.

That first indoor game showed some key innovations to the sport. By moving the game inside, the number of players became restricted to nine on each team. Until then, the size of the outdoor rink had determined how many players could fit on the ice. Players

also used a puck for the first time and had much more control over this flat wooden disk than the lacrosse ball they had earlier used.

In 1877, James G. A. Creighton — who was a captain during that early indoor game — would publish the first official set of rules, and the McGill University Hockey Club would become the first organized hockey team.

1876 The Indian Act

By the late 1800s, there was a growing rift between Aboriginal peoples and European settlers. The government of Canada stepped in to take control and introduced the Indian Act in 1876. The goal of this act was to assimilate Aboriginal people — to make them give up their traditional ways and blend into the non-Aboriginal population.

Over the years, the Indian Act was amended (changed) 42 times. For example, when Aboriginal people began raising money to hire lawyers to defend their claims to the lands, the Indian Act was amended. They now required the government's permission to hire lawyers.

Aboriginal people who refused to renounce their official Aboriginal status were denied certain rights, such as the right to a high school education, to vote, to buy land or to serve on juries. The act went so far as to deny Aboriginal people the right to use fish weirs (traps), to own powerboats and to sell fish.

Rather than assimilating Aboriginal people, the act made Canada into a two-tiered system based on race. Aboriginal people who refused to give up their "Indian" status became wards of the government with few rights, while other Canadians were citizens and had full rights.

The Indian Act is still in force today, although its fate remains uncertain. Most Aboriginal people agree that the Indian Act has not served their people well. However, while some are fighting for self-government, others still see a role for the Canadian government in Aboriginal affairs. There are many different views on the best path to the future.

1877 Treaty Number 7

Between 1871 and 1921, Aboriginal peoples in the Prairies signed 11 treaties (formal agreements) with the British government. Treaty Number 7 was signed in 1877 and is one of the most famous because it concerned one of the largest areas of land.

The Canadian government promised Aboriginal peoples money and a place to live, in exchange for land in southern Alberta (which wasn't yet part of Canada). Chief Crowfoot of the Siksika First Nation knew nothing could stop the spread of European settlers. He and the other chiefs agreed to the treaty.

Canada's government did not meet the treaty's terms. Treaty Number 7 is still the focus of much discussion between Aboriginal peoples and the government.

1878 Women practice medicine

Like other women who tried to study medicine in Canada more than 150 years ago, Emily Jennings Stowe found the doors of Canadian universities closed. She was definitely smart enough — in 1852, she'd become Canada's first female school principal. So Emily went to the United States and graduated as a doctor in 1867. That still didn't allow her to practice medicine legally back home, but she opened an office in Toronto anyway and became the first woman to practice medicine in Canada.

In 1870, the Toronto School of Medicine reluctantly admitted Emily and another woman, Jennie Trout, so that they could complete their studies. The male professors and students made Emily's and Jennie's lives difficult, so Emily left the school. Jennie persevered, and in 1875, she became the first Canadian woman to earn a medical license.

By 1878, both Emily and Jennie were practicing medicine in Toronto. (Emily eventually earned her license in 1880.) To make it easier for other women to become doctors, Emily opened the Woman's Medical College in 1883. Emily's daughter, Augusta Stowe-Gullen, was so inspired by her mother that in 1883 she graduated from the Toronto School of Medicine — the first woman to take her entire medical training in Canada.

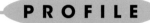
PROFILE

Leonora Howard King

Her desire to be a doctor took Leonora Howard King away from Canada. Smart and determined, Leonora headed to the United States to study medicine, like Emily Jennings Stowe, and graduated with honours in 1876. She sailed to China the next year, looking for adventure and a chance to spread Christianity as a missionary. In China, Leonora treated both royalty and people with little money — often for free. For her work, she was made a mandarin (similar to a knight). She was the first North American woman to earn such a rare honour from China.

1879 Standard Time proposed

When the first transcontinental railway was planned between Montreal and the Pacific Ocean in 1871, Sandford Fleming was the engineer in charge. His energy, intelligence and desire to unite Canada made him perfect for the job. (In 1863, he had been the chief surveyor of the railway built between Quebec City and Saint John, New Brunswick.)

But when the railway began running across Canada, there were problems timing the trains. Back then, everyone told time by the sun. Noon occurred when the sun was directly overhead. So noon in one town wasn't necessarily noon in another town. In fact, at one point, there were 144 "official" local times in North America.

The different local times caused railway accidents, and many passengers had to carry several watches. So Sandford proposed Standard Time in 1879, a system that would divide the world into just 24 time zones.

At first, the idea was rejected, but Sandford was committed and kept pushing for it. Standard Time eventually came into use around the world on January 1, 1885. The railway companies (and passengers) were especially grateful.

1880 "O Canada!"

On June 24, 1880, people crowded onto the Plains of Abraham in Quebec City for the Saint-Jean-Baptiste Day celebrations. As part of the festivities, three bands struck up a new anthem written for the occasion — "O Canada!" with words by Judge Adolphe-Basile Routhier and music by Calixa Lavallée.

The crowd was silent as the words of the great song rolled over them: *"O Canada! Terre de nos aïeux, Ton front est ceint de fleurons glorieux …"* When it was finished, the crowd applauded long and loud. "O Canada!" was a hit — in French. Various English translations were tried, and in 1908, the English version by Robert Stanley Weir caught on. But it wasn't until July 1, 1980, that "O Canada!" officially became the country's national anthem.

1881 Canadian Pacific Railway

Canada's first prime minister, Sir John A. Macdonald (page 7), had a dream of a strong nation that stretched from the Atlantic Ocean to the Pacific. To entice British Columbia to join the young country, he promised to build a railway that would connect the west coast to the rest of Canada.

The Canadian Pacific Railway (CPR) company was formed in 1881, and a route for the ribbon of steel across the country was chosen. Construction began that year with the first spike (a large nail to fasten down railway tracks) being hammered in place at Bonfield, Ontario. But by the end of the construction season, only 211 km (131 mi.) of track had been built.

The chief engineer was replaced with William Cornelius Van Horne (page 15). By the final day of the next season, Cornelius's workers had laid 673 km (418 mi.) of main-line tracks, as well as branch lines.

Construction was also under way from the west, but laying track through the mountains of Alberta and British Columbia was difficult. It took expert surveyor Major Albert Bowman Rogers two seasons to find a pass that the railway could use through the Selkirk Mountains. It was named Rogers Pass in his honour.

About 30 000 labourers, called navvies, worked on the railway. These included Chinese men (page 16) who were brought to Canada for the job. They built strong bridges to span British Columbia's raging rivers and deep canyons.

Laying track through the mountains was very expensive, and by 1885, the CPR had run out of money. But when the North-West Rebellion (pages 18–19) broke out in Saskatchewan in March 1885, the nearly completed railway was used to quickly move soldiers from eastern Canada to the western area in less than 10 days. That showed how useful the railway was, and the CPR received a loan from the government to finish laying the track.

On November 7, 1885, the railway was completed, six years ahead of schedule. That morning, at Craigellachie, British Columbia, CPR co-founder Donald Smith drove in the last spike, signalling the completion of the CPR. When it was finished, it was the longest railway in the world — about 3200 km (2000 mi.) long — and had been built faster than anyone had thought possible.

The CPR changed Canada. Entire cities, such as Winnipeg and Moose Jaw, sprang up near the stations along its gleaming rails as new businesses, including hotels and farm suppliers, flooded in. The railway brought settlers to new homes in the Prairies and united the vast country from coast to coast.

PROFILE

William Cornelius Van Horne

By 1881, it was clear that building the railway was tougher than anyone had thought. The CPR needed someone who really knew railways, so the company hired William Cornelius Van Horne. He'd started working around railways in Illinois when he was 14, and he loved and understood the business.

Cornelius divided the route across the country into sections and had teams of workers start in different places. The workers had to cross deep gorges, treacherous swamps, the rugged Rocky Mountains and other tough terrain, but by 1885, the job was done. Cornelius became president of the CPR in 1888 and worked hard to make the company grow. When he died, the CPR halted all trains for a whole day.

1882 Chinese railway workers

To get the Canadian Pacific Railway (pages 14–15) built, the railway company used workers from China. Between 1881 and 1884, about 17 000 Chinese men came to Canada. More than 8000 of these men arrived in 1882.

The Chinese workers often faced discrimination. They were paid less than other workers, earning under a dollar a day, and had to live in cold, drafty tents separate from the workers with European backgrounds. Some of the other workers thought that the Chinese men were taking jobs away from others, and so they became resentful.

The Chinese immigrants had left their families in China and were eager to send back as much money as possible. To earn extra money, many of the Chinese railway workers took on tough, dangerous jobs, such as clearing and levelling the railway's track bed and lighting

explosives to blast tunnels through rock. More than 600 railway workers from China died building the railway. Some of their families were never told what happened.

When the Chinese workers were no longer needed to help build the railway, Canada decided to limit immigration from China. The government introduced a head tax, which was a fee Chinese immigrants had to pay to come to Canada. No other nationality had to pay this tax. In 1885, the head tax was $50, and it was raised to $500 in 1903. The head tax ended in 1923, but other laws that almost stopped all Chinese immigration were in place until 1947. Finally, in 1967, these restrictions were lifted.

In 2006, the government apologized for the way Chinese immigrants had been treated and paid compensation to the survivors and their families.

1883 Timothy Eaton's store

Timothy Eaton changed the way Canadians shopped. In 1869, he opened a store in Toronto based on three promises: fixed prices, cash only and satisfaction guaranteed or money refunded.

What a difference! Up to then, shoppers and store owners would haggle over dollars and cents, but "fixed prices" meant everyone knew the cost. "Cash only" put an end to bartering for goods and gave the shop owner more money to pay the bills. And "satisfaction guaranteed or money refunded" gave the buyer peace of mind — if the goods were faulty, the store promised to take them back.

By 1883, business was booming, and Timothy opened a three-storey store on Yonge Street. This light, airy workplace had many modern innovations, including indoor washrooms, electric lights and an elevator.

But Timothy wanted to sell to even more people, including those living outside of Toronto. So in 1884, he put out a mail-order catalogue. It became known as the "Farmer's Bible." People shopped from the Eaton's catalogue — and also used it for hockey shin pads, insulation and toilet paper!

1884 *Albertosaurus*

In 1884, a young geologist named Joseph B. Tyrrell stumbled across a huge animal skull embedded in a riverbank near Drumheller, Alberta. He dug it out and sent it to Ottawa. There, it was identified as a new type of dinosaur — later named *Albertosaurus* — that had lived 70 million years ago. Today, you can see *Albertosaurus* skeletons at the Royal Tyrrell Museum of Palaeontology, named after the dinosaur's discoverer.

"*I stuck my head around a point and there was this skull leering at me, sticking right out of the ground. It gave me a fright.*"

— Joseph B. Tyrrell

CANADA GROWS 1885–1899

At the end of the 1800s, Canada was still growing. By 1885, the population was already 25 percent larger than it had been when the country formed in 1867. The Klondike Gold Rush brought so many people to Canada's north that in 1898, the Northwest Territories was split to form the Yukon Territory.

That year, cars became more widely available in Canada, although most people still travelled by horse and carriage. In cities, many middle-class homes now had indoor plumbing.

The railway continued to expand, and many men headed west to work on the rail line. In Ontario, a new law stated that children had to attend school. However, some children whose families had little money had to work on farms or in factories rather than go to school.

As the country grew, so did the conflict between the Canadian government and the Métis in Manitoba and farther west. This would eventually lead to rebellion.

1885 North-West Rebellion

After Confederation, Prime Minister Sir John A. Macdonald wanted to expand Canada from the Atlantic Ocean to the Pacific. That chance came in 1869, when the Hudson's Bay Company agreed to sell its vast territory in the north and the west. But no one discussed the sale with the people who were living on the land. When the Métis in the Red River area, around today's Winnipeg, heard about it,

they decided they must act. They were worried that they would lose their culture, their Catholic religion and their land.

The Métis chose Louis Riel as their leader because he was well educated, as a priest and a law clerk. He led his people through the Red River Rebellion (1869–1870), during which the Métis wrote up a "List of Rights" that protected their land and customs. He had also been heavily involved in the creation of Manitoba as a province in 1870, which included territory reserved for the Métis. Louis was elected to the House of Commons (the part of Parliament made up of elected politicians) three times between 1873 and 1874.

Louis was banished from Canada for five years, from 1875 to 1880, for his part in the Red River Rebellion. During those years, he had a nervous breakdown and spent time in a psychiatric hospital. He also became obsessed with religion. In June 1884, Louis was working as a teacher in Montana when a group of Saskatchewan Métis asked him to return to Canada and help them stand up for their rights.

On March 18 and 19, 1885, Louis and the Métis set up a provisional (temporary) government at Batoche, Saskatchewan. About a week later, a group of Métis and First Nations people fought the first of several battles against the North-West Mounted Police (NWMP) in the North-West Rebellion.

After a fight at Fort Pitt in mid-April, 5000 government troops arrived. They far outnumbered the Métis and First Nations fighters and were much better equipped. For instance, during the Battle of Batoche, the Métis ran short of ammunition. They dug enemy bullets out of walls to reuse them and even fired buttons, nails and rocks.

Louis was forced to surrender on May 15, 1885, after being defeated in the Battle of Batoche. The North-West Rebellion ended less than three weeks later. He was tried in court and sentenced to death. Three times the execution was postponed, but finally Louis was hanged at Regina, Saskatchewan, on November 16, 1885.

These events in the west, and Louis's hanging, caused a huge divide among Canadians. People still argue about him. To some, he's a hero because he defended the Métis and helped make Manitoba part of Canada. To others, Louis is a traitor because he started two rebellions.

North-West Rebellion, 1885

March 26	Led by expert hunter Gabriel Dumont, the Métis defeat the NWMP at Duck Lake (near Batoche).
March 30	Starving First Nations people attack Battleford.
April 2	First Nations people defeat the NWMP at Frog Lake (north of today's Lloydminster).
April 15	The NWMP are beaten by First Nations people at Fort Pitt (near the Alberta border).
April 24	Métis hold their ground against government troops at Fish Creek (near Batoche).
May 2	First Nations win at Cut Knife Hill (near Battleford).
May 9–15	The Battle of Batoche between Métis and government soldiers ends in defeat for the Métis.
June 3	Cree fighters lose to NWMP soldiers at Loon Lake (near Fort Pitt). This is the last battle of the rebellion and the last battle fought in Canada.

1886 First passenger train

In late 1885, the eastern and western portions of the Canadian Pacific Railway (pages 14–15) had met in Craigellachie, British Columbia. Finally, Canada had a railway that linked its mainland provinces.

On June 28, 1886, the first passenger train left Montreal, and it arrived on July 4 in Port Moody, British Columbia (now part of Vancouver). It had taken the train's 150 passengers 5 days and 19 hours to make the trip — but they arrived on time.

That first train included two first-class coaches for wealthy passengers, as well as a second-class coach. There was also a sleeping car, where passengers making long journeys could rest, as well as a mail car. The dining car, where passengers could buy meals, was detached during the night and another one picked up in the morning. Passengers ate off fine china with silverware.

In addition, there was a colonist car, the most basic and cheapest type of coach for settlers heading west. These cars had hard wooden benches and uncomfortable platforms, known as berths, where the settlers slept — they had to bring their own blankets. Only the first-class cars had washrooms, so other passengers had to wait until the train stopped at a railway station!

Riding the Cowcatcher

In July 1886, Canada's prime minister, Sir John A. Macdonald, and his wife, Agnes, rode one of the first trains to cross the country. Just west of Banff, Alberta, Lady Agnes decided to travel the rest of the trip to the west coast on the train's cowcatcher. These metal bars on the front of the train push away anything — even cows — blocking the tracks. "It is all so delightful," said Lady Agnes about her incredible ride.

1887 First national park

When three railway workers found hot springs on an Alberta mountainside in 1883, the federal government decided the area should be set aside for public use. A park, now called Banff National Park, was established two years later. In 1887, a law was passed that made it the first national park in Canada. Today, there are more than 40 national parks across the country.

1888 Soccer tour in Britain

In August 1888, a group of Canadian soccer players headed to Britain. In a gruelling schedule of 23 games over just 61 days, they played against the best teams of Ireland, Scotland and England.

The Canadians earned a record of nine wins, nine losses and five ties. However, four of those losses came in the last four games. By then, the Canadians were exhausted and injured. But one magazine wrote, "They have taken down some big clubs and quite surprised a host of people."

In 1998, a 50-cent coin was issued to commemorate this tour. Today, soccer is one of the fastest-growing sports in Canada.

1889 Women fight for the vote

In the 1800s, women in Canada weren't allowed to vote. Although they paid taxes, they couldn't choose the people who decided how to spend the tax money. That didn't seem fair to many Canadian women.

So in 1889, Emily Jennings Stowe formed the Dominion Women's Enfranchisement Association (DWEA). (Dominions are countries with connections to Great Britain, and *enfranchisement* means the right to vote.) Emily knew about fighting for women's rights thanks to her efforts to become the first woman to practice medicine in Canada (page 13).

Canada's women used humour and persistence to fight for their rights. In 1896, Emily and her daughter, Augusta Stowe-Gullen, staged a mock parliament where women debated whether *men* should be given the vote. They repeated the arguments men had used against letting women vote. In the end, the "members of parliament" decided not to allow men to vote.

The DWEA encouraged and inspired Canadian women, many of whom were granted the right to vote in 1918 (page 37), although Aboriginal women could not vote until 1960 (page 63).

1890 Manitoba Schools Question

To bring an end to the Red River Rebellion of 1870 (pages 18–19), the Canadian government passed the Manitoba Act. This act created the province of Manitoba. As well, it stated that French and English were equally important in the new province and provincial laws had to be printed in both languages.

The act also created two school systems in Manitoba, one for Protestant students and one for Roman Catholic students. Back then, almost all Protestants in Manitoba spoke English and practically all Catholics spoke French. So the Protestant schools provided education in English, and the Catholic schools taught in French.

But by 1890, more and more English-speaking Protestants were coming to Manitoba. The Manitoba government decided to create one public school system. Since the language of the schools was English, some people believed the new system was really for Protestants. Some parents still wanted to educate their children in Catholic schools. Since these schools were no longer funded by the government, the parents had to pay school fees.

Catholics and French Canadians across Canada saw this as an attack on their rights. The Manitoba Schools Question became a countrywide issue during the 1896 federal election. The Liberal Party won the election because its leader, Wilfrid Laurier, said he could negotiate a compromise that would satisfy both sides. Eventually, it was decided that schooling in French and for Catholics could be available if enough families requested it.

The Manitoba Schools Question was a language and religion issue. It was also a battle about the roles of federal and provincial governments. These were important issues in the late 1800s — and still are today.

1891 Basketball is invented

Canadian James Naismith had just 14 days to invent a game for his students in Springfield, Massachusetts, when they couldn't exercise outside. He tried indoor soccer, football and lacrosse, but all were too dangerous to play in such a small space.

James's new idea began with a large ball. Players would have to pass the ball, not run with it. The goal would be up high so the players couldn't block it with their bodies. Any rough conduct would earn a penalty. Each team had nine players, to include all the students in the class.

The students tested the new game in December 1891. James nailed up a peach basket at either end of the gym. Each time a player tossed the ball into the basket, the game had to stop while the janitor retrieved the ball. Even so, the players loved the game. Eventually, someone decided to cut the bottoms out of the baskets.

James didn't have a name for his game at first. Some of the students suggested Naismith-ball, but he came to prefer another name: basketball.

Did You Know?

James Naismith originally asked for boxes to be nailed up as goals in his game. Can you imagine playing "boxball"?

1892 Father of Modern Medicine

William Osler transformed the way medicine is taught, not only in Canada but around the world. Until the late 1800s, medical students spent most of their time in lecture halls or labs and rarely saw sick people. William thought that student doctors should learn from patients, so he increased the hours of patient-student contact.

William also gave lessons at the bedsides of sick people because he knew this was an effective way of training students. His students learned from him how important it is to listen carefully to the patient when making a diagnosis.

Besides being an excellent teacher, William was also an expert in diagnosing diseases of the heart, lungs and blood. Friendly and outgoing, he knew how to inspire his patients with hope. He had a good sense of humour and liked to play practical jokes on friends.

In 1892, William wrote a medical textbook that was used

for more than 40 years. He also helped create the system of training for new doctors that's still followed today. By the end of the 1800s, William was one of the best-known doctors in the world. He would eventually become known as the Father of Modern Medicine.

"We are here to add what we can to life, not to get what we can from it."

— William Osler

1893 Stanley Cup

It's the oldest trophy awarded to professional athletes in North America. Today, millions of hockey fans watch the National Hockey League (NHL) play-offs each year to see who will win the Stanley Cup.

The award is named for Lord Stanley, who was Governor General of Canada from 1888 to 1893. He and his family came from England and quickly became hockey fans. Stanley's sons

persuaded him to donate a sterling silver bowl to Canada's best hockey team. The cup was first awarded in 1893 to the Montreal Amateur Athletic Association.

The Stanley Cup later inspired Governor General Earl Grey to donate a trophy for Canada's football league, and the Grey Cup was created in 1909.

1894 Carnaval de Québec

In the early 1890s, the North American economy was suffering. Quebec City was especially hard hit with the closing of its shipyards. Frank Carrel, owner of the *Quebec Daily Telegraph*, decided a winter festival would help.

The first Quebec Winter Carnival, or the Carnaval de Québec, was held in 1894. The mascot Bonhomme Carnaval, a huge snowman, first appeared at the festival in 1955.

Today, more than 600 000 people attend the carnival each year — it's the world's largest winter carnival. You can see parades, ice sculptures and sports such as dog sledding, ice canoeing and snowboarding.

1895 Strongman Louis Cyr

In 1895, Louis Cyr lifted a platform on his back holding 18 large men — a weight of 1967 kg (4336 lb.). With one finger, Quebec's strongman could lift 272 kg (600 lb.)!

Louis worked as a lumberjack and police officer before he became a weightlifter. Feats of strength were extremely popular in his day, and Louis took part in many challenge matches. Once, a horse was tied to each of his huge arms, but no matter how hard the horses tried to drag Louis in opposite directions, he was able to hold them at a standstill.

1896 Yukon gold

Gold was discovered in August 1896 at Rabbit Creek, later named Bonanza Creek, in the Yukon Territory, but the rush didn't start until 1897. That year, near the Klondike River, prospectors found gold in large flakes that they could pick easily from the rocks.

Almost overnight, thousands of people headed north hoping to get rich. Most sailed up to Skagway, Alaska, then had to trek inland through the Coast Mountains to the goldfields. White Pass and Chilkoot Pass were the most popular routes through the mountains.

Prospectors pitched their tents in Dawson near the goldfields. With them came saloon keepers, merchants and the North-West Mounted Police. In 1898, Yukon became a federal territory with Dawson as the capital city.

By 1899, the gold that could be found easily was almost gone. Dawson shrank as quickly as it had grown. By 1900, only companies with expensive equipment could look for gold.

1897 Canadian film

Canada's first filmmaker was Manitoba farmer James Freer. In 1897, he filmed scenes of trains and prairie farm life for his film *Ten Years in Manitoba*.

In 1902, Canada's first permanent movie theatre opened. Magician and showman John Schuberg rented a store in Vancouver and showed the movie *Mt. Pelee in Eruption and Destruction of St. Pierre*. It was about a volcano erupting on the Caribbean island of Martinique.

Today, Canadian filmmakers such as David Cronenberg, Atom Egoyan (page 91), Deepa Mehta and Sarah Polley (page 93) continue to make stories about Canada come alive for moviegoers around the world.

1898 WP&YR railway

When the Klondike Gold Rush began in 1896 (page 24), thousands flooded into the Yukon Territory. Businesspeople quickly realized miners would pay to ride a train to Whitehorse, now Yukon's capital. Construction began on the White Pass and Yukon Route (WP&YR) in May 1898.

By the time the WP&YR was completed in July 1900, the gold rush was over. So the WP&YR carried ore from Klondike mines to Skagway, Alaska. During World War II, the line hauled materials to help construct the Alaska Highway. The rail line shut down in 1982 when the mines closed. In 1988, the WP&YR reopened as a rail line for tourists.

1899 Women practice law

Clara Brett Martin became the first woman lawyer not only in Canada but in the whole British Empire. She succeeded in 1897 only after she had challenged and changed the laws that prevented women from studying law. In 1899, she opened her first practice. Despite a very successful career as a lawyer, Clara rarely appeared in court because her presence caused such a commotion.

Even though women could become lawyers after 1897, it wasn't until 1976 that an Aboriginal woman, Roberta Jamieson, became a lawyer in Canada. A dynamic Mohawk leader and chief of the largest reserve in Canada, she works hard for better relations between the government and Aboriginal peoples.

A NEW CENTURY 1900–1913

As the country moved into the 1900s, Canadians were full of hope. More than five million people were living across the country, and by 1914, another three million immigrants had settled in the Prairies. Gold and other minerals were being mined in the north.

Most Canadians lived on farms, not in cities. Many of those farms had no running water, no indoor bathrooms and no electricity. Women who held jobs outside their homes or farms mostly worked as maids, cooks and cleaners.

By the end of the 1800s, kids across Canada had to attend school. Since more Canadians could now read, newspapers were the most popular way to keep up with the daily news — there was still no radio or television.

Prime Minister Sir Wilfrid Laurier said, "I think the twentieth century shall be filled by Canada." Most Canadians agreed that the new century would be a great one for their country.

1900 Battle of Paardeberg

By the end of the 1800s, Canada was at peace for the first time in many years. But wars still raged elsewhere in the world. When Britain got involved in a war in 1899 over rights for a group of settlers (called Boers) in faraway South Africa, Canada was asked to help.

About 8000 Canadians volunteered in the South African War, and Britain agreed to pay their salaries. Some of these soldiers replaced British soldiers who were stationed in Halifax, so they could take part in the war overseas. Others went to South Africa to fight.

The Canadian volunteers arrived in Cape Town, South Africa, at the end of November 1899. They spent two months training and learned new techniques for fighting off surprise attacks. This skill would prove to be useful in the battles to come with the Boers.

The Battle of Paardeberg in February 1900 marked the first time large numbers of Canadian troops saw battle overseas. The battle lasted nine days and was the biggest, bloodiest fight of the whole war.

Towards the end of the battle, the Canadians tried to surprise the Boer forces by attacking before dawn. But the 4000 Boers soon had the raiders under heavy fire. The soldiers from Canada were told to retreat, but two companies from the Maritimes — each with only about 125 men — kept firing.

Finally, the exhausted Boers surrendered. The Canadians had won the battle. One of the British commanders remarked, "*Canadian* now stands for bravery, dash and courage."

1901 Wartime nurses

When the South African War broke out in 1899, four nurses sailed overseas with the first troops. By 1901, it became clear that more nurses were needed. The Canadian Army Nursing Service was created that year, and additional nurses were sent to help.

Georgina Pope volunteered to serve in the South African War and was one of the first military nurses to go overseas. The conditions were horrible. Despite epidemics and shortages of food and medical supplies, Georgina and the group of nurses she led saved many lives. In 1903, she became the first Canadian to be awarded the Royal Red Cross medal.

Soon, Georgina was made head of the Nursing Service for the Canadian Army Medical Corps. She went on to train nurses for World War I and served in France during that war. Because of her, people began to think of nurses as skilled professionals.

1902 South African War ends

For more than two years, Canadian soldiers fought in South Africa. News of battles at Zand River, Mafeking, Lydenburg and Harts River was reported in Canadian newspapers. At Leliefontein, 90 Canadians were assigned to protect retreating British soldiers. The Canadians managed to hold off several hundred Boers.

In May 1902, Britain and its contingents won the South African War. In the end, 224 Canadians had died, and 252 had been wounded. Four Canadians won the Victoria Cross, Britain's highest military award. These soldiers fought while wounded or while incredibly outnumbered.

Another Canadian private was nominated twice for a Victoria Cross but never received the medal. Instead, he received a scarf that was knit by Queen Victoria herself, which was a great honour.

1903 Harriet Brooks Pitcher's theory

It was unlikely that Harriet Brooks would study science at university. Not only did she live at a time when it was difficult for women to get an education, but she also came from a family that had little money. But Harriet was a good student and won scholarships. In 1894, she began studying at McGill University in Montreal.

Harriet graduated in 1898 and a year later began researching radioactivity, a new field in science. She studied radioactive elements (an element is a substance made up of only one kind of atom) and proved that one element could change into another, something scientists had thought impossible. While doing this work, she helped identify the element radon.

In 1903, Harriet discovered that when a radioactive atom ejects a particle, the atom springs back, or recoils. This became known as the "recoil theory" of atoms and is still important today. From 1906 to 1907, she worked with Marie Curie, who was then the only woman physicist more famous than Harriet.

Harriet married Frank Pitcher in 1907, and as for many women at the time, marriage ended her work in science. But she had accomplished more during her short career than many scientists do in a lifetime.

1904 First Olympic team

When Canadian athletes competed in the 1904 Olympics, it was the first time Canada had sent an official team to the games. The Olympics were held in St. Louis, Missouri, and were spread out over more than four months.

In ancient Greece, Olympic Games took place from 776 BCE to 393 CE. In 1896, the Olympics were restarted, but no Canadians took part in those games. At the games held in 1900 in Paris, athletes competed as individuals, rather than as part of a team representing a country.

Canada won four gold medals at the 1904 games, in golf, soccer, lacrosse and track and field. George Lyon won his gold medal in golf after competing against 76 players — all from the United States!

Another Canadian gold medalist was Étienne Desmarteau, a police officer from Montreal.

He was fired from his job when he left to compete at the games. But when Étienne placed first in track and field's 25 kg (56 lb.) weight throw event, he returned home a hero — and got his job back!

Canada also took home the silver medal in rowing and the bronze medal in lacrosse (the country had two lacrosse teams competing that year!).

Did You Know?

Before the 1904 Olympics, a silver medal was awarded for first place, and a bronze for second. Third-place finishers received nothing.

1905 Settlement of the Prairies

In 1896, Sir Wilfrid Laurier became prime minister. Hoping to fill the West with settlers, his government advertised throughout Europe, promising good farmland and great opportunities. People poured in — from Ukraine, Poland, Germany, Norway and many other places.

Some got a horrible shock when they saw where they were to live. It was often just a flat stretch of prairie — nothing but grass as far as the horizon. A settler's first home was usually a flimsy shack or a sod house made of turf. But farms and ranches were soon started, and towns sprung up to supply them.

Between 1900 and 1914, nearly three million people poured into the Prairies. By 1905, immigration was in full swing. That same year, the provinces of Alberta and Saskatchewan were formed. Both soon had a network of railways to take wheat and other products to distant markets. So much wheat was grown that Canada was called "the breadbasket of the world."

The wheat boom was the result of two Canadian developments — new types of farm machinery and a new type of wheat. Much of the machinery was made by Massey-Harris, the largest farm-equipment company in the British Empire. The wheat was called Marquis and had been bred by Charles Saunders. It did well in the Prairies because it ripened faster than other wheat.

1906 Wireless radio broadcast

When radio waves were first used by Guglielmo Marconi to transmit sound, all you could hear were the clicks of Morse code. It was Quebec-born Reginald Fessenden who fine-tuned the radio to broadcast voices. He made his first wireless radio broadcast on December 24, 1906, from his base near Boston. Reginald sang Christmas carols and played his violin, reaching merchant ships far down the Atlantic coast.

Guglielmo Marconi

Like telegraphs, early telephones needed wires. Imagine the excitement when, in 1895, a young Italian inventor named Guglielmo Marconi found a way to send messages without wires. He used radio waves to send Morse code. In a famous test of the new technology on December 12, 1901, Guglielmo sent and received the world's first transatlantic Morse code messages, from England to Signal Hill in St. John's, Newfoundland.

1907 Cars made in Canada

Before cars were invented, people in Canada used horse-drawn carriages and sleighs to get around. Robert Samuel McLaughlin knew these vehicles well, having designed more than 140 models while working at his father's factory.

Sam got his first ride in an automobile in 1904. It had no doors, top or windows, so when it rained, passengers got soaked! The car owner asked Sam to design something to help keep passengers dry. Sam made a cover for the car, and as a thank you, the owner let him drive the automobile.

Travel and speed had always fascinated Sam, and he was soon hooked on cars.

In 1907, in Oshawa, Ontario, Sam set up the McLaughlin Motor Car Company, with himself as president. This was the first major car manufacturer in Canada — the company created the first car assembled in Canada. Sam sold his company to the General Motors Company in 1918 but stayed on as president.

Now a rich man, Sam believed in sharing his wealth. One of his main interests was Canadians' health, so he supported medical research. He also helped many arts, education and community groups.

1908 *Anne of Green Gables*

Anne of Green Gables, Emily of New Moon, Pat of Silver Bush — these are just a few of the wonderful children's books that sprang from the pen of Lucy Maud Montgomery. She wrote 24 books, 530 short stories and more than 500 poems during her lifetime. In the process, she introduced her beloved Prince Edward Island and Canada to the world.

Maud — she hated being called Lucy — was a schoolteacher, but she spent her spare time writing short stories and poems. Later she earned a living from these, but she longed to write a book. That seemed like an impossible dream, until Maud got an idea for a wonderful character — a red-haired orphan named Anne. It took Maud months to write Anne's story, fitting it in between her other writing and chores.

Maud proudly sent off her manuscript to a publisher. But it quickly came back rejected. That happened four more times! Maud was very discouraged and put the story aside for a few months. Then she decided to send it out one last time. Finally, Maud's manuscript was accepted, and on June 20, 1908, Maud opened the package that held her first book, *Anne of Green Gables*.

Today, Maud's books are read around the world. *Anne of Green Gables* has been published in more than 20 languages and has sold tens of millions of copies.

"I believed in myself and I struggled on alone, in secrecy and silence. I never told my ambitions and efforts and failures to anyone."

— Lucy Maud Montgomery

1909 Airplanes take off!

In 1876, Alexander Graham Bell became world-famous for his invention of the telephone (page 11). But when he was a boy, he had dreamed of flying like a bird. So in 1891, Aleck, as he was called, began experimenting with flight.

These first experiments used kites that were big enough to carry a person. Most of the experimenting was carried out at Aleck's home in Baddeck, Nova Scotia.

Aleck was disappointed when the Wright brothers became the first people to fly in 1903. However, he kept working on his own design for a flying machine — he called it an aerodrome. His wife, Mabel, gave him the money to hire four young men to help him build it. Together they formed the Aerial Experiment Association (AEA).

The men began testing out various designs. They quickly moved from kites to gliders, which are aircraft that have no engines but use the wind for power. Then the AEA began building biplanes — planes with two sets of wings. To help steer, they added adjustable flaps, called ailerons, to the wings. Today's planes still have this hinge system.

On February 23, 1909, the AEA tested its most successful plane. The airplane sped through the air like a dart and had a silvery, waterproof coating on its wings, so it was named the *Silver Dart*. This was the first airplane flight in Canada and the British Empire.

PROFILE

Tom Longboat

Spectacular finishing sprints made Thomas Longboat one of the world's greatest runners. He could summon a burst of energy at the end of a long race when his competitors could barely stay on their feet. In 1909, he won the World's Professional Marathon Championship, defeating the world's best runners.

Born on the Six Nations reserve in Brantford, Ontario, Tom could take over any race he ran, but off the track, his life was tough. He often had fights with his managers over his training. He faced criticism and racist insults because he was an Aboriginal person. But nothing slowed him down — he just kept winning. Because of his skin colour and swiftness, he came to be known as the "Bronze Mercury." Mercury is the Roman god of travel and the gods' messenger who has wings on his heels.

Burgess Shale Fossils

One of Canada's most famous fossil finds was made in 1909 at Mount Burgess in the Rockies. Scientists uncovered fossils of thousands of ancient sea creatures in shale (a type of sedimentary rock) at the top of the mountain. This great diversity of life included sponges and sea worms, as well as the first animals that developed eyes, mouths, guts, gills, pincers, jointed legs, shells and backbones.

These creatures thrived along the muddy sea banks surrounding Laurentia, a land mass near the equator that

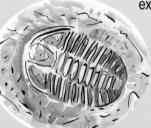

existed more than 500 million years ago. They died in a mudslide, trapped at the bottom of the sea. Around 300 million years later, they resurfaced, preserved in rock, 2500 m (8200 ft.) above sea level and thousands of kilometres away from where they once swam.

Some scientists say that the whole animal kingdom, including humans, can trace its ancestry back to the creatures of the Burgess Shale. It is one of the most important scientific sites in the world!

1910 First chocolate bar

In 1910, the first chocolate bar in North America was developed at the Ganong chocolate factory in St. Stephen, New Brunswick, as a quick snack for fishermen. It was created by James and Gilbert Ganong, who had opened a grocery store in 1873. They soon realized that they needed to sell something special to stay competitive, so they began making sweets. Today, St. Stephen is known as "Canada's chocolate town" and even has a chocolate museum!

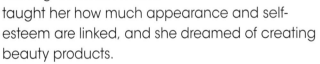

PROFILE

Elizabeth Arden

Named after the most famous nurse in history, Florence Nightingale Graham of Ontario seemed destined to become a nurse. But when she tried nursing, the young Florence soon found she was too squeamish for the job. Still, her training with burn victims taught her how much appearance and self-esteem are linked, and she dreamed of creating beauty products.

Florence began making skin creams in her kitchen. Some of them smelled like rotten eggs, but she didn't give up. In 1910, she opened her own beauty salon in New York and gave herself a new name — Elizabeth Arden. Women flocked to the salon. Until then, makeup was usually worn only on stage, but by the 1920s, Elizabeth helped make it available to everyone. She also introduced eye makeup to North America. Today, her products are sold around the world.

1911 Parks Canada

Parks Canada was set up in 1911 and was the world's first national parks service. It was created to protect wilderness areas, while making it possible for Canadians to visit and appreciate them. Because the parks were hard to get to, only rich people could afford to visit them. But Parks Canada wanted to make parks available to everyone. The organization increased the number of parks and created them across the country.

Also vital to Parks Canada are national historic sites, including forts and places important to Aboriginal peoples. As well, Parks Canada set up the National Landmarks Program in 1978 to protect rare natural features such as the pingos (mounds of soil-covered ice) in the Northwest Territories.

In 2002, Parks Canada started the National Marine Conservation Areas Program to protect coastlines. These sites include Gwaii Haanas in British Columbia, Lake Superior in Ontario and Saguenay–St. Lawrence in Quebec. Today, Parks Canada manages 44 parks, 167 national historic sites, 4 national marine conservation areas and 1 national landmark.

Did You Know?

Wood Buffalo National Park is Canada's largest national park. On the border between Alberta and the Northwest Territories, it's bigger than Switzerland!

1912 Calgary Stampede

The Calgary Stampede is a 10-day celebration of the rodeo skills — such as bronc riding, steer wrestling and calf roping — that were needed in early ranching days and are still in use today.

The first stampede was held in 1912, after vaudeville performer Guy Weadick dreamed of holding a world-class rodeo competition. Both men and women competed that year. It wasn't until 1923 that the stampede became an annual event. Today, the Calgary Stampede is an important part of the city's culture and history, welcoming over a million visitors from across Canada and around the world every year.

1913 Arctic exploration

When the Canadian Arctic Expedition went north in 1913, it was the first time the government had sent explorers to the western Arctic. The 14 researchers and scientists came from the world's top universities to study the area's animals, plants and rocks.

The extreme cold made it a difficult journey. The ships became frozen in the ice, and 11 crew members died before the expedition ended in 1918.

The group discovered five islands that had been unknown even to the Inuit. These explorers asserted Canada's control over a vast area. However, countries still argue today over who owns the Arctic (page 85).

WARTIME AND BEYOND 1914–1928

When Britain declared war on Germany in 1914 and entered World War I, Canada was automatically at war. Canada was still a British dominion, so Britain decided how Canada dealt with other countries.

Tensions later developed in Canada over conscription (mandatory participation by men in the war). Some Canadians felt this was a British war and didn't want to take part. But conscription became the law and men were forced to fight.

The roles of Canadian women changed as many women took over men's jobs while the men were away fighting. Women also looked for a solution to the problem of alcohol, and by early 1918, Prohibition — a law banning alcohol — was in effect. This wartime sacrifice was seen as a patriotic duty.

When World War I ended in late 1918, Canada was a more confident nation. In the conference held in 1919 to negotiate the war's end, Canada gained greater recognition when it attended as an independent nation.

1914 World War I begins

The assassination of Archduke Franz Ferdinand of Austria-Hungary in June 1914 triggered World War I. On one side were the Central Powers: Austria-Hungary and Germany (and later Turkey and Bulgaria). On the other side were the Allies: France, Russia, Great Britain and countries in the British Empire, including Canada. Later, Italy, Japan and the United States joined the Allies. Canadians thought the war would end quickly. But they had four long years of fighting ahead.

Life in the Trenches

During World War I, soldiers on both sides dug trenches to protect themselves from advancing enemy troops. These trenches were zigzagging passages cut deep into the ground along the front of the battle lines in some areas of Belgium, France and northern Italy. For weeks at a time, the soldiers would fight, eat and sleep in the trenches.

Rain filled the trenches with cold, muddy water. Adding to the misery was a painful infection called trench foot, which soldiers got from standing in the muck.

Weary soldiers had only a few days off. During this break, they could visit a nearby town, eat a good meal and leave the horrors of war and the trenches behind for a little while.

1915 Second Battle of Ypres

One of Canada's early battles during World War I was on April 22, 1915, at Ypres in Belgium. This was the first time the Germans used chlorine gas in war. It spread in a yellow-green cloud, blinding and suffocating the French soldiers on the front lines. As the gassed men retreated, the Canadians rushed in and held back the Germans.

Two days later, the Germans attacked Canadian soldiers with gas. The Canadians soaked their handkerchiefs with muddy water or urine and held them over their faces. Despite the Germans' heavy shelling, the Canadians managed to stop them.

The fighting continued at Ypres for more than a month. About 6000 Canadians died or were wounded.

FIRST

After seeing Allied troops attacked by poison gas, Newfoundlander Cluny Macpherson invented the first gas mask in 1915. Macpherson took a helmet and added a hood made of fabric treated to absorb the gas. The hood also had eyepieces and a breathing tube. It would become the war's most important protective device.

PROFILE

John McCrae

World War I was a nightmare for John McCrae. Although he had been a doctor for many years and had already served in the South African War, in this war dead and dying soldiers surrounded him. Every day, he cared for hundreds of wounded men — but he couldn't get used to their terrible suffering.

The day after burying a friend on a battlefield in Belgium, John realized that even though he couldn't help his friend or other dead soldiers, he could tell of their lives in a poem. He could see blood-red poppies blowing in the wind in a nearby cemetery, and they inspired him to write "In Flanders Fields."

John didn't think the poem was very good and threw it away. But an officer found the poem and sent it to magazines and newspapers in England, where it was published on December 8, 1915.

Because of John's poem, the poppy became the flower of remembrance for many countries, including Canada.

John died of pneumonia at a battle hospital in 1918. His poem was used on billboards in Canada to raise money for the war effort, and $400 million (more than $6 billion in today's dollars) was collected — almost three times the hoped-for amount. "In Flanders Fields" is still recited around the world on Remembrance Day each year.

In Flanders fields the poppies blow
Between the crosses, row on row,
That mark our place, and in the sky
The larks, still bravely singing, fly
Scarce heard amid the guns below.

— from "In Flanders Fields"

1916 Battle of the Somme

The Battle of the Somme, named after a river in northern France, was one of the longest and bloodiest battles of World War I. It established Canadian soldiers' reputation for courage and determination when leading an attack. As well, it marked the first time tanks were used on the battlefield.

The battle started on July 1, 1916, and continued for more than four months. Because of the constant barrage of gun shells and bullets, the Canadians advanced slowly and at great human cost. More than 24 000 Canadians were killed or injured during the Battle of the Somme.

1917 Battles of Vimy Ridge and Passchendaele

During World War I, the British and French had tried several times to take Vimy Ridge in northern France but failed. In April 1917, it was Canada's turn to make an attempt. The attack was scheduled to begin at dawn. That meant the soldiers had to lie out in the trenches all night. Falling drizzle chilled the men to the bone. At Vimy, the British shelled the Germans, clearing the way for the advancing Canadians. Thirty thousand Canadians wrestled Vimy Ridge out of German hands. These brave soldiers gained more ground and captured more German guns and prisoners than in any previous Allied attack on the Western Front.

While Vimy Ridge would be one of Canada's great victories of the war, that same year would also see one of the war's most devastating battles. The Battle of Passchendaele took place in Belgium. By October 1917, German and British soldiers had been fighting there for weeks. It had rained relentlessly, and by the time the Canadians were ordered in, the mud was waist deep in some places. The mud swallowed soldiers, guns and supplies. Wounded men drowned in it. For more than two weeks, the Canadians struggled to take Passchendaele from the Germans. It was a major victory, but almost 16 000 Canadians died or were injured in the fighting.

Beaumont Hamel

While most Canadians celebrate Canada Day on July 1, for many people in Newfoundland and Labrador, it is a time of great sadness. On that day in 1916, the Newfoundland Regiment suffered extreme losses. The Allies had planned an attack at the village of Beaumont Hamel on the Somme River, to break the Germans' front line. But the Germans were well prepared. Of the 801 members of the Newfoundland Regiment, only 68 escaped injury — the rest were killed, wounded or missing.

Halifax Explosion

Halifax Harbour was crowded with ships during World War I. On the morning of December 6, 1917, the Belgian ship *Imo* accidentally hit the *Mont Blanc* from France. The French ship was packed with explosives, and it blew sky high in the biggest human-caused explosion up to that time. Much of the north end of Halifax was destroyed by the blast, and by the tidal wave and fire that followed. More than 1600 people died, and 9000 were injured.

1918 The Hundred Days

The last three months of World War I became known as the Hundred Days. Canadian soldiers had incredible successes on the battlefields, starting with the Battle of Amiens on August 8, 1918. There, Canadian and other Allied soldiers broke through the German lines and advanced 13 km (8 mi.) in one day. Canadians and the Allies went on to attack enemy fortifications known as the Hindenburg Line and captured more than 30 000 soldiers. The war was drawing to a close.

Germany finally surrendered, and World War I ended on November 11, 1918. This war became known as the Great War because it affected so many people. Some 625 000 Canadians enlisted in the war. More than 61 000 died and another 172 000 were wounded.

Women Get the Vote

By the turn of the century, women were taking a bigger part in public life. Some were members of the suffrage movement, which aimed to get women the right to vote. Only men could vote, though some women had voted in Lower Canada (the southern part of today's Quebec) until a law in 1834 had stopped them.

The suffrage movement was strong in the Prairies, where Nellie McClung was an activist. The Prairie provinces were the first to give women the vote, beginning with Manitoba in January 1916. That year, Emily Murphy was elected as the first woman magistrate in the British Empire.

Women's contributions to World War I, at home and overseas, helped to strengthen the suffrage movement. In 1917, the Wartime Elections Act gave the vote to female relatives of soldiers. The Military Voter's Act granted the vote to women serving in the war. By the end of the war, in 1918, most women had the right to vote in federal (countrywide) elections.

In 1921, Agnes Macphail was elected to Parliament in the first federal election where women could vote.

WOMEN'S FRANCHISE MATTERS
COME TO ST. JAMES'S HALL
AT 8:30 O'CLOCK
FREE TO ALL

When Women Got the Vote in Provincial/Territorial Elections

1916	Manitoba, Saskatchewan, Alberta
1917	British Columbia, Ontario
1918	Nova Scotia
1919	New Brunswick, Yukon Territory
1922	Prince Edward Island
1925	Newfoundland (later Newfoundland and Labrador)
1940	Quebec
1951	Northwest Territories (Nunavut was part of the Northwest Territories until 1999)

1919 Winnipeg General Strike

Since 1872, it had been legal for Canadian workers to form unions to negotiate better working conditions. But factory workers and miners still worked long days and earned little money. When Canadian soldiers returned home after World War I, they felt they had the right to ask for higher pay, safer working conditions and shorter workdays.

In Winnipeg on May 15, 1919, negotiations broke down between management and workers in the building and metal trades. The Winnipeg Trades and Labour Council called for all workers to go on strike to support the labourers.

Within hours, almost 30 000 people left work in what would become the largest strike in Canadian history. Streetcars stopped, postal and phone communications halted and other strikes broke out across Canada. Winnipeg business leaders asked the federal government for help. The North-West Mounted Police were sent in to keep order.

"Don't worry and don't work."
— *Western Labour News*

The strike continued for more than a month. On June 21, a crowd of 6000 gathered at Winnipeg's city hall. When a streetcar, driven by non-striking workers, approached the group, they overturned it and set it on fire. The mounted police charged the crowd, killing 2 people and injuring more than 30.

The strikers went back to work on June 25, 1919, because they wanted to end the violence. But the Winnipeg General Strike inspired other groups across Canada to walk out to protest their working conditions. However, it would be more than 30 years before Canadian unions were truly accepted as a means to protect workers.

1920 Group of Seven

Between 1911 and 1913, a group of young men began to paint together. Franklin Carmichael, Lawren Harris, A. Y. Jackson, Frank (later Franz) Johnston, Arthur Lismer, J. E. H. MacDonald, Tom Thomson and F. H. Varley shared an idea for a new style of painting that captured Canada's spirit. Most of them earned money during the week by designing posters and ads. But on weekends and holidays, they explored Canada's wilderness, creating small sketches with oil paints, from which they created their larger, final paintings.

These artists used bright colours and rough brushstrokes to show how different Canada was from other countries. They knew they were doing something unusual, so in 1920, they decided to show their art in a group exhibition, figuring that might help people accept it. They decided to call themselves the Group of Seven. (Tom Thomson had died in a canoe accident in 1917, leaving just seven artists.)

The group's first exhibition in Toronto that year caused a huge commotion. One critic called the group the "Hot Mush School" because he thought the paintings looked more like porridge than art. Others liked the fresh new way the group pictured Canada.

The Group of Seven painted to show not only how parts of Canada looked but also how these natural areas made them feel. With a new sense of confidence and independence after World War I, Canadians

soon accepted these artists who made such strong paintings of the country they loved.

As members left the group, other painters — A. J. Casson, L. L. FitzGerald and Edwin Holgate — joined. Today, you'll find paintings by Group of Seven members in every major gallery in Canada.

1921 Coat of arms

The coat of arms is one of Canada's official symbols. The current design was adopted on November 21, 1921, at the same time that red and white became Canada's national colours.

The shield in the middle represents Canada's earliest European settlers with the three royal lions of England, the royal lion of Scotland, the royal Irish harp of Tara and the royal fleurs-de-lis of France. The three maple leaves represent Canadians of all origins.

The lion on the left holds the British flag, and the unicorn on the right holds the royal flag of France. They stand on Canada's motto: "A Mari usque ad Mare" (From Sea to Sea). A gold lion holding a maple leaf is above, symbolizing valour and courage. At the very top is the imperial crown. Below are the French fleur-de-lis, the Irish shamrock, the Scottish thistle and the English rose.

1922 Snowmobile

When Joseph-Armand Bombardier was a child, driving through snow in his hometown of Valcourt, Quebec, was tough. Since Joseph-Armand loved working on machines and was good at it, he and his brother Léopold decided to create a vehicle to carry people over the snow. In 1922, when Joseph-Armand was just 15, the brothers attached a car motor and an airplane propeller to a sleigh. The boys amazed the neighbours with their snow machine.

After training as a mechanic, Joseph-Armand opened a garage in 1926 and spent his spare time experimenting with snow vehicles. He developed a machine with steerable skis and a set of caterpillar tracks, and in 1937, he produced a vehicle that could carry seven people over snow.

Joseph-Armand was also a clever and creative businessperson, and he dreamed of inventing a smaller machine for one or two people. In 1959, he created the Ski-Doo snowmobile. It changed how people got around in winter, especially in the Arctic, and created a whole new winter sport.

Did You Know?

Joseph-Armand Bombardier originally called his invention the Ski-Dog, since it was meant to replace dogsleds. After a brochure misprinted it as Ski-Doo, Joseph-Armand decided to keep the new name.

1923 Frederick Banting's Nobel Prize

In 1921, Charles Best had just finished his degree in biochemistry and physiology (sciences that study how living organisms work) when his boss at the University of Toronto, Professor John Macleod, gave him the opportunity to work on experiments with Frederick Banting. Charles leaped at the chance — Frederick was trying to find a treatment for diabetes, a deadly disease. Little did Charles know that this work would make him famous years before he became a doctor.

Doctors knew that diabetes was caused by the lack of a hormone called insulin. But they couldn't figure out how to supply needed insulin to patients. Frederick had an idea, and he was determined to make it work. He and Charles tried injecting diabetic dogs with an insulin solution.

James Collip, the other key team member, purified the insulin they used. When the dogs were treated with the insulin, they improved.

In 1922, insulin was successfully tested on a human. This was a major medical breakthrough, and the team won many awards. Frederick Banting and John Macleod won the Nobel Prize for Medicine in 1923, and Frederick shared his prize money with Charles. While insulin isn't a cure, it helps control diabetes and has saved the lives of millions of people around the world.

Did You Know?

Charles had to toss a coin with a classmate to decide who would start working with Frederick. Luckily for Charles, he won the toss!

Canadian Nobel Prize Winners

1923	Frederick Banting — Physiology or Medicine
1957	Lester B. Pearson (page 61) — Peace
1966	Charles B. Huggins — Physiology or Medicine
1971	Gerhard Herzberg — Chemistry
1981	David H. Hubel — Physiology or Medicine
1983	Henry Taube — Chemistry
1986	John Polanyi — Chemistry
1989	Sidney Altman — Chemistry
1990	Richard Taylor — Physics
1992	Rudolph A. Marcus — Chemistry
1993	Michael Smith — Chemistry
1994	Bertram Brockhouse — Physics
1995	Pugwash Conference on Science and World Affairs — Peace
1996	William Vickrey — Economics
1997	Myron Scholes — Economics
1999	Robert Mundell — Economics
2009	Willard Boyle — Physics
2009	Jack W. Szostak — Physiology or Medicine
2011	Ralph M. Steinman — Physiology or Medicine
2013	Alice Munro (page 87) — Literature
2015	Arthur B. McDonald — Physics

1924 Pier 21

Pier 21 was a dock in Halifax, Nova Scotia, where ships arrived after crossing the Atlantic Ocean from Europe. Immigrants began arriving there in 1924, although the pier didn't officially open until 1928. The site became known as the Gateway to Canada. People wanting to move to Canada landed there, then met with government officials. Before being allowed into the new country, immigrants were checked by doctors for infectious diseases. They also had to speak to immigration officials, who reviewed travel documents and made sure no one was a criminal.

A lot of the people who were accepted to stay in Canada had no idea what to do next. Some couldn't speak English or French. Volunteers helped the immigrants with the difficult step of starting a new life in a new country. Pier 21 facilities included a kitchen, dining room, nursery, hospital and dormitory.

Immigrants brought as much as they could from their old homes. Many even tried to

bring food into Canada, which was generally not allowed. Sausages were the most common food people tried to bring in. Immigrants were often given free cornflakes as a gift when they arrived at Pier 21, but they had never seen the cereal before and had no idea what to do with it!

Many of the British home children (page 10) arrived in Canada at Pier 21. When Canada entered World War II in 1939 (page 50), Pier 21 was immediately taken over by the Department of National Defence. More than 500 000 Canadian soldiers left from Pier 21 to cross the ocean and take part in the war in Europe. Many of them married women in Great Britain or France. After the war, these war brides came to Canada and passed through Pier 21, too.

Over the years, hundreds of ships brought immigrants to Pier 21. More than one million immigrants entered Canada through this important gateway. But by 1971, more immigrants were arriving in Canada by plane than

by boat, and fewer and fewer ships arrived at Pier 21. The facility closed that year.

In 1999, the site reopened as the Canadian Museum of Immigration. There you can watch videos about some of Canada's immigrants, see artifacts and exhibits about their journeys and hear people's incredible stories about entering Canada through Pier 21.

FIRST

In 1924, the first synchronized swimming competition was held at the YMCA in Montreal. Originally called ornamental or scientific swimming, it was developed by Peg Seller for women who didn't want to speed swim.

Canadian swimmers have since won many gold medals in synchronized swimming — maybe because the sport is a Canadian invention.

1925 Climbing Mount Logan

A team of Canadian, British and American mountaineers assembled to reach the summit of Mount Logan — Canada's tallest mountain — for the first time in 1925. Located west of Whitehorse, Yukon, the mountain is named after Sir William Edmond Logan, a Canadian geologist (a scientist who studies the earth) and founder of the Geological Survey of Canada — Canada's oldest scientific agency.

The expedition had been planned since 1922, but it took a long time to get funding, plan the ascent, scout out a base camp and haul in supplies. Finally, in May 1925, the climbers were ready.

It may not be the world's tallest mountain (and it's only the second-tallest in North America), but Mount Logan's freezing temperatures and fierce storms can make it tough to climb. In places, the snow can be 300 m (984 ft.) deep.

On June 23, 1925, the climbing team finally reached the top of Mount Logan. They had to spend that night high on its bitterly cold slopes when a severe storm suddenly swept the mountain. The expedition took 65 days, but all of the climbers returned home safely.

Did You Know?

Mount Logan has 11 peaks and measures 5959 m (19 550 ft.) high, but because of how Earth's tectonic plates shift, it's still growing!

1926 King-Byng Affair

In October 1925, William Lyon Mackenzie King was Canada's prime minister and leader of the Liberal Party. However, an election had just given the Conservative Party 116 seats in the House of Commons and William's party just 101. William was able to stay on as prime minister with the support of the Members of Parliament (MPs) from other parties, including Progressive, Labour and Independent MPs.

At the time, Prohibition (a law banning alcohol) was in effect in certain provinces and in the United States. But some Canadian customs officers were accepting bribes from criminals smuggling liquor into America. The bribery became public, and in June 1926, a majority of MPs called for a vote to show that the government couldn't be trusted. William knew his party would lose. So he asked Governor General Lord Julian Byng to dissolve, or end, Parliament and call an election. The Governor General said no.

This was the first time a Canadian Governor General had refused the request of a prime minister to dissolve Parliament. William resigned. Arthur Meighen, leader of the Conservatives, became prime minister, but his government was defeated just days later by the Liberals and the other MPs.

An election was called, and William's party won. Up to this time, the Governor General had represented the king or queen of Canada, as well as the British government. After the election, William's party soon changed the role of the Governor General to represent only Canada's monarch (king or queen), not the British government. No other Governor General has ever refused to dissolve Parliament.

1927 Emily Carr's exhibition

When Emily Carr was growing up, painting was considered a nice hobby for proper young ladies but not a serious career choice. Emily, however, longed to paint, especially the lush landscapes of British Columbia's west coast.

She was most inspired by Kwakiutl First Nation villages. Emily headed out alone by boat to paint village houses and totem poles. On one visit to Ucluelet, on the west coast of Vancouver Island, she was given the name Klee Wyck, which means "Laughing One."

Painting didn't earn Emily enough money to live on, so she rented out rooms in her house in Victoria. Being a landlady took up a lot of time, leaving less for painting. But Emily didn't give up.

It wasn't until 1927, when Emily was 56, that people really started to notice her art. That year, she was invited to show her work at an exhibition at the National Gallery of Canada in Ottawa, where she met members of the Group of Seven (page 38), who encouraged and helped her. Their inspiration motivated her to paint forests, shorelines and skies that shimmered with light and energy.

Emily loved animals and was always surrounded by dogs, cats, birds and even a pet monkey named

Woo. During the summer, she would head off with her pets to her trailer (which she called The Elephant) to be closer to nature and create her art.

In 1937, Emily had a heart attack and was told to cut back on her painting. So she began writing — and became an award-winning author. Her books are published in more than 20 languages around the world. But Emily is best known for her art. She is still Canada's most famous female artist, and her paintings hang on gallery walls across the country.

1928 Bobbie Rosenfeld wins gold

When Fanny "Bobbie" Rosenfeld went to the Olympics in 1928, it was the first year Canadian women competed in the games. Bobbie ended up winning gold and silver in track and field, and scored more points than any other athlete — male or female. She led the small Canadian women's team (nicknamed the Matchless Six) to first place.

Bobbie's sports career started early. While at a picnic as a child, she and her sister lost their lunch money. A kids' race was being held with lunch as the prize.

Bobbie was determined to win — and did.

In her early years as an athlete, Bobbie competed all over Ontario, often wearing her brother's shorts and her dad's socks. She stunned other competitors and wowed fans when she won first and second prizes in sports she'd never before competed in. Tennis, hockey, track, softball — Bobbie excelled at them all.

Bobbie would go on to win many awards and championships, but by 1933, severe arthritis ended

her sports career. She became a sportswriter, known for her wit and strong support of women's rights.

In 1949, she was named Canada's top woman athlete of the first half of the 1900s.

Did You Know?

In 1900, George Orton became Canada's first Olympic gold medalist. He won for the steeplechase — an obstacle race with a water pit!

THE GREAT DEPRESSION 1929–1938

The 1930s were tough times for Canadians. The Great Depression hit the country harder than most because Canada depended so much on trading with other nations. The price of important exports, such as lumber and cattle, fell drastically. To make matters worse, Prairie farmers were hit by droughts and swarms of grasshoppers that ate their crops.

Canadians did what they could to help one another. People in wealthier provinces sent food and clothing to the impoverished farmers in Saskatchewan. Prime Minister R. B. Bennett even sent some of his own money to anyone who mailed him a letter asking for help.

Canadians cheered themselves by listening to radio programs or, when they had a quarter to spare, going to the movies to watch musicals and comedies. Through entertainment, they were able to briefly escape these dark times.

1929 Persons Case

Today, Canadian women can be elected or appointed to all parts of Parliament: the House of Commons, the Senate and as Governor General. They gained these rights thanks to the determination and dedication of the Famous Five: Henrietta Muir Edwards, Nellie McClung, Louise McKinney, Emily Murphy and Irene Parlby.

These five were well-educated women working in Alberta to improve women's lives. They fought to establish a minimum wage for women, to increase farm women's rights and to improve people's health, especially in frontier areas. All five women felt it was their responsibility to make changes in society so that everyone was treated fairly and equally.

It was because of Emily Murphy that the Famous Five came together. In 1916, on Emily's first day on the job as a magistrate (a type of judge), a lawyer told her that she had no right to be there. According to the British North America (BNA) Act, he said, a woman was not a person. Later, when women's groups were pressuring government to make Emily a senator, she faced the same argument — that a woman couldn't be appointed to Canada's Senate because she wasn't a person.

"Whenever I don't know whether to fight or not, I fight."

— Emily Murphy

Emily got tired of being told that the law said she wasn't a person. She found out that she needed a group of five to challenge this ruling. So in 1927, the Famous Five joined together and sent a petition to the Supreme Court of Canada — the top law court in the country — asking if the word "person" in the BNA Act included female persons. The court debated for five weeks and decided that, no, women were not included.

The Famous Five were shocked, but didn't give up their fight. They took the Persons Case, as it became known, to the Privy Council of England, Canada's highest court at that time. On October 18, 1929, the Privy Council declared "that the exclusion of women from all public offices is a relic of days more barbarous than ours." Finally, women were legally persons and so could hold any appointed or elected office.

1930 Mary Pickford's Academy Award

Making films was not something teenage stage actor Gladys Louise Smith wanted to do. She felt movies were second-rate. But when she got a chance to audition for a movie that paid much better than her stage work in Toronto, she changed her mind since she desperately needed the money. She also changed her name — to Mary Pickford — and went on to become a movie star, and then a superstar. In the 1910s and 1920s, Mary was one of the most famous women alive.

Mary was able to quickly adjust her acting style to suit the movies, and audiences loved the spunky characters she played. She soon became known as America's Sweetheart.

At a time when most women didn't have jobs or careers, Mary earned as much as $350 000 per movie, a huge amount then. By age 24, she was Hollywood's

first-ever millionaire. When movie studios could no longer afford Mary's salary, she and other movie superstars joined together to start their own studio, United Artists, in 1919.

Mary won her first Academy Award in 1930 for the movie *Coquette*, and won an Academy Honorary Award in 1976 for her contribution to the film industry. But more important, she changed how people thought about independent women.

"The past cannot be changed. The future is yet in your power."

— Mary Pickford

PROFILE

Cairine Wilson

When Cairine Wilson became the first Canadian woman appointed to the Senate in 1930, there was a lot of opposition. Most people thought Prime Minister William Lyon Mackenzie King should have chosen Emily Murphy instead because she worked to make women eligible to become senators (page 44). As well, many of the male senators didn't want a woman in the Senate.

Cairine suspected that in return for her appointment, the prime minister would expect her to go along with his government's proposals. But Cairine was tough and wasn't afraid to disagree with him.

As chairman of the Canadian National Committee on Refugees from 1938 to 1948, Cairine worked hard on behalf of refugees and immigrants. Her interest in people from other countries led to her appointment as Canada's first woman delegate to the United Nations, in 1949.

1931 Statute of Westminster

The Statute of Westminster of 1931 decreed that Canada and other countries in the British Commonwealth were equal partners with Great Britain and had the right to make their own laws.

Canada had been making its own laws for years, but Britain generally had a say in Canada's relations with other countries. In 1923, Canada passed a treaty with the United States, and for the first time Britain was not involved. Once the Statute of Westminster was passed in 1931, Canada officially had the right to manage its own affairs, abroad as well as at home.

1932 Superman

When 17-year-old Joe Shuster sketched the first Superman in 1932, the character was very different from the superhero we know today. The cartoonist had teamed up with his friend Jerome Siegel to create a series of comics, and in 1933, they published a comic featuring a villain named Superman who wanted to take over the world. Later that year, the pair reworked the character into a hero named Clark Kent who had a secret identity.

Superman's fictional city of Metropolis was based on Joe's hometown of Toronto, and the *Daily Planet* — the newspaper where Clark Kent works — was based on the *Toronto Daily Star*, which Joe delivered as a kid.

In 1938, Joe and Jerome sold their character to Action Comics. Superman went on to become a major hit and paved the way for many more action heroes.

"... a strange visitor from another planet with powers and abilities far beyond those of mortal men."

— Joe Shuster's original idea for Superman

1933 The depth of the Great Depression

The economic crisis known as the Great Depression began in 1929. Throughout the world, banks lost money, factories and businesses closed and millions of people lost their jobs.

Farmers in the Prairies got hardly any money for their wheat. Worse still, so little rain fell during the 1930s that many farmers couldn't grow any crops. Their fields turned into clouds of blowing dust.

By 1933, the country was at the depth of the Great Depression with nearly one-third of people out of work. Unable to afford gasoline, some people used farm animals to pull their cars. They called these vehicles "Bennett buggies," blaming Prime Minister R. B. Bennett for their poverty. He spent large sums trying to end the Depression. But with so many people out of work, Bennett couldn't solve the problem. Neither could the next prime minister, William Lyon Mackenzie King.

It wasn't until 1939, with the start of World War II, that the country's economy started to recover.

1934 Dionne Quintuplets

The Dionne Quintuplets were the world's first surviving quintuplets — five babies born at the same time — when they were born on May 28, 1934. Up to 6000 people a day came to watch Annette, Cécile, Émilie, Marie and Yvonne play at "Quintland" close to their home near North Bay, Ontario.

Did You Know?

By 1943, nearly three million people had visited Quintland. It had become Ontario's biggest tourist attraction — beating out even Niagara Falls!

1935 Bank of Canada

For years, the Bank of Montreal, Canada's largest bank, had also been the bank for the government of Canada. But in 1935, the government decided to create a separate central bank.

The Bank of Canada is owned by the government and is its banker. This bank issues paper currency (bills or banknotes).

Coins are produced by the Royal Canadian Mint.

During World War II, the Bank of Canada helped pay for the war effort. Since then, its job has been to encourage economic growth in Canada, mainly by controlling the rate of inflation (the rise in prices over time) and keeping Canada's money secure.

Did You Know?

The *Bluenose*, a famous racing and fishing schooner, appears on the Canadian dime. It symbolizes the country's fishing industry and maritime history.

1936 CBC is formed

In 1936, the Canadian Broadcasting Corporation (CBC) was formed so that people across the vast country could stay in touch through live radio broadcasts. Receiving daily news was particularly important during the Great Depression.

Prime Minister R. B. Bennett helped to form the CBC, and he spoke directly to Canadians through the radio — something no other prime minister had ever done. He let people know about his plans for minimum wage and unemployment insurance, which would help support them through hard times.

Today, the CBC broadcasts in French and English and beams programs in Aboriginal languages to the Arctic by satellite.

> *"Canadians have a right to a system of broadcasting from Canadian sources equal in all respects to that of any other country."*
>
> — R. B. Bennett

Globe and Mail

In 1936, another important media company was formed — the *Globe and Mail*. The newspaper was created when George McCullagh merged the *Globe* with the *Mail and Empire*. Today, more than two million people read the *Globe and Mail* every week for news about Canada and the rest of the world.

1937 Glenn Gould composes music

At age three, Glenn Gould could already read music. He began to compose in 1937 when he was just five. By fourteen, he was performing as a solo pianist with the Toronto Symphony Orchestra, and within a few years, he was one of Canada's most important musicians.

Glenn performed all over the world, and his performances were legendary. He sat in a low, rickety-looking chair, humming or singing along (you can hear him on some of his recordings) and conducting himself. People made such a fuss over these unusual habits that in 1964, Glenn stopped performing in public. He even came to be known as a bit of a hermit.

But Glenn continued to record music — especially by composer J. S. Bach. He made more than 60 recordings, cutting and splicing until he had the most perfect version he could make. Glenn also appeared in several films and television shows. He even created radio programs, including one about his favourite part of Canada, the Far North.

1938 Norman Bethune in China

When Henry Norman Bethune was just eight, he stuck on his bedroom door the nameplate that had belonged to his surgeon grandfather. It seemed he was already on his way to a medical career.

Norman served in Europe during World War I, carrying wounded men on stretchers. He was shipped back to Canada when he, too, was badly wounded. While recovering, he got his medical degree and began treating patients. But in 1926, Norman became ill with tuberculosis (a lung disease). He was sure he was going to die from it — as many people did — until he read about a possible surgical treatment for the disease. Norman arranged to try it, and it cured him, so he learned how to perform the surgery himself.

Norman became well known as a surgeon specializing in diseases of the chest, heart and lungs. The shears he invented for cutting ribs were so well designed that they're still used today.

When civil war in Spain broke out in 1936, Norman was asked to head a medical team there. While treating wounded patients, he invented a mobile blood bank that could be wheeled onto the battlefield. He performed blood transfusions in the midst of battle and saved many lives.

Norman left for China in 1938, where he would live until his death the following year. He is best known for the work that he did there — treating Chinese soldiers during a war with Japan and training many Chinese people as doctors. Norman's accomplishments have saved lives all over the world.

RETURN TO WAR 1939–1953

When World War II began in 1939, Canadians felt a new sense of responsibility. Canadian soldiers headed overseas to fight as they had in World War I, and some women once again took over the jobs left by men. There were many other changes on the home front. Food rationing made feeding families difficult, but it was important to send lots of food to the hard-working soldiers.

As in World War I, Canadians fought bravely and earned the respect of countries around the world. When the war ended in 1945, industry was booming and Canada's economy improved. People's tastes changed from military-themed movies and practical clothing to romantic films and extravagant fashion styles, including large wide-brimmed hats and dresses with full skirts.

Canada returned to war in 1950, when North Korea invaded South Korea. The United Nations sent in a special force and almost 27 000 Canadians enlisted to fight.

1939 World War II begins

After World War I, people's memories of the horrors of war were still strong. It seemed impossible that Canada would go to battle again. But when German troops under their leader, Adolf Hitler, invaded Poland in 1939, that changed.

Germany was joined by such countries as Italy and Japan, and they became known as the Axis Powers. Fighting them were the Allies, including Britain, France, Australia, New Zealand, South Africa and Canada. (Russia and the United States would join later.) Canada was not automatically at war as it had been when Britain joined World War I (page 34), but independently declared war on September 10, 1939.

Battle of the Atlantic

Throughout the war, German submarines, called U-boats, attacked ships bringing supplies and aircraft to Britain from North America. Canadian corvettes (escort ships) and aircraft, based out of Newfoundland and the Maritimes, protected the supply ships. This battle at sea would become known as the Battle of the Atlantic, which started in 1939 and lasted for the entire war.

By the time the war ended, more than 25 000 supply ships would cross the Atlantic safely. The Canadian navy and air force would sink nearly 50 of the 1100 enemy submarines destroyed by the Allies. About 2000 Canadians in the navy and 1600 in the merchant marine (commercial cargo and passenger ships that helped the navy) would die trying to protect Allied ships.

1940 Battle of Britain

The first Canadian soldiers arrived in England in December 1939, ready to fight. But nothing much happened. People started calling it the Phony War because neither side launched any big attacks in the first months of 1940. Then Germany invaded Denmark and Norway in April, and France, the Netherlands and Belgium in May. Canadians landed in France in June ready to fight, but they were forced to retreat.

In the summer of 1940, Germany began attacking England — from the air. The Battle of Britain was the first battle in world history to be fought exclusively with planes. There were only a few hundred Allied fighter pilots at that time, and about a hundred of them were Canadian. But some of the Canadians had never even fired at a moving target. By the end of October 1940, 23 Canadian pilots had given their lives to stop the Germans.

British Commonwealth Air Training Plan

One of Canada's biggest contributions to the war was the British Commonwealth Air Training Plan (BCATP). This was a program to train aircrews from Australia, Canada, Great Britain and New Zealand, as well as occupied European countries. Canada was the perfect place for this program: it had wide-open skies and was far from possible enemy attacks, but close enough to Britain to supply aircrew quickly when needed.

The first course in Canada began in 1940. At its peak, there were 107 training schools for pilots and 184 other training sites across Canada. When the program ended in 1945, it had produced more than 130 000 bomb aimers, gunners, pilots, navigators and wireless operators. Today, the Commonwealth Air Training Plan Museum at the airport in Brandon, Manitoba, commemorates this important contribution to the war.

1941 Battle of Hong Kong

World War II didn't take place just in Europe. In December 1941, Japan bombed Pearl Harbor, Hawaii, which brought the United States into the war. Then Japan launched attacks throughout Southeast Asia. Soon, the Japanese were targeting Hong Kong and Singapore, which belonged to Britain at the time.

Almost 2000 inexperienced Canadians, along with British and Indian soldiers, were sent to defend Hong Kong. They took on the tough Japanese army in mid-December 1941, but on Christmas Day, they had to surrender. More than 550 Canadians were killed or died in cruel prisoner-of-war camps.

1942 Battle of Dieppe

By 1942, the war was going badly for the Allies. The Germans occupied France, and German soldiers were also forcing their way into Russia. To test the German defences and take pressure off Russia, the British decided to attack Dieppe, a French coastal town held by the Germans.

The huge attack on August 19 involved at least 6000 Allied soldiers. And it was a nightmare. The Germans learned of the attack ahead of time. They were ready for the soldiers who disembarked from ships on the beach at Dieppe. The raid occurred in broad daylight, so the Allied soldiers were easy to spot. The Allied tanks were useless — the beach was covered with large pebbles. On all sides, the Germans kept firing.

About 5000 Canadians were part of the attack on Dieppe — more than 3400 were captured, wounded or killed. People still argue about why the raid ended in such disaster. The next time the Allies attacked France's coast (page 54), they would not make the same mistakes.

Did You Know?

By November 1942, German submarines had sunk 18 ships on Canada's east coast. Canada then improved its defences on the home front.

Japanese-Canadian Internment

During the war, Canada's government treated Canadians of Japanese descent very badly since they were believed to be a threat. That's because Japan, which was an Axis Power along with Germany and Italy, attacked the United States in an air raid on Pearl Harbor in Hawaii on December 7, 1941. The next day, Japanese soldiers attacked the British garrison at Hong Kong, where some Canadian soldiers were stationed.

Since British Columbia is the part of Canada closest to Japan, some Canadians feared a Japanese invasion. So the Canadian government took action. By September 1942, about 22 000 Japanese Canadians in British Columbia had their homes and businesses taken away. Anything they couldn't carry with them was also seized and later sold.

Some Japanese Canadians were taken to internment, or imprisonment, camps in the interior of British Columbia. They were crowded into tents or shacks that often had no electricity or running water.

When the war ended, Japanese Canadians were not allowed to stay in British Columbia. Almost 4000 left for Japan. Most who stayed in Canada moved to Ontario, Quebec or the Prairies. None were ever paid back for all that had been taken from them.

It wasn't until 1988 that the Canadian government finally apologized to Japanese Canadians. The government also had imprisoned Canadians of German and Italian descent during World War II. In 1990, the prime minister apologized to Italian Canadians.

1943 Italian Campaign

When the Allies invaded the island of Sicily, Italy, in 1943, Canadians were there. They fought over incredibly rough countryside, earning a reputation for toughness. The battle took 38 days, but the Allies eventually established a base for moving to Italy's mainland.

In miserable winter weather in Ortona and in summer heat in Rimini, the Canadians battled through machine guns and land mines, and they kept advancing. About 93 000 Canadians served in Italy, and 5400 lost their lives.

PROFILE

The Carty Brothers

During World War I, most black Canadian soldiers had had to fight in segregated units. But in World War II, they fought alongside other soldiers in mixed regiments. Five of the seven sons in the Carty family of Saint John, New Brunswick, served in the war. Adolphus, Clyde, Donald, Gerald and William all joined the air force. They all survived the war and returned home to Canada. The youngest Carty brothers, Malcolm and Robert, were members of the army and air cadets at home.

Women at War

About 45 000 Canadian women enlisted in World War II. Approximately 5000 went overseas and saw duty in the Women's Royal Canadian Naval Service, the Canadian Women's Army Corps and the Royal Canadian Air Force Women's Division. Canadian women weren't allowed to fight but instead held other jobs, such as drivers, mechanics and radar operators. More than 4000 Canadian women also served bravely as nurses in many countries, including Belgium, Britain and France.

On the home front, at least 261 000 women built guns, aircraft and other equipment. Women who didn't serve during the war or work in war-related industries still made major contributions. They knitted, prepared bandages, wrote letters to soldiers and collected scrap — bones, fat, metal and rubber — that could be made into ammunition and tanks.

Women also collected money for the war through Victory Loan drives, which raised billions of dollars for the war effort. Kids bought war savings stamps to help out.

1944 D-Day and the Normandy Invasion

For their next European invasion, the Allies spent months training soldiers and planning. Just after midnight on June 6, 1944, the day ever after known as D-Day, Allied airplanes and ships began bombarding the Germans stationed on the north coast of France, in the region of Normandy.

At dawn, more than 100 000 soldiers — including 15 000 Canadians — began pouring out of troop-carrying ships. Canadians landed on the beach between Vaux and St. Aubin-sur-Mer — an area code-named Juno Beach. They had to cross the open beach under heavy German gunfire.

Those who made it ashore ended up fighting in the streets of the nearby French towns. Some Canadians faced special units of German soldiers known for their ruthlessness. By the end of D-Day, Canadians had advanced 9 km (6 mi.) inland — farther than any other Allied soldiers. However, the victory cost 340 Canadians their lives. Another 574 were wounded, and 47 were taken prisoner.

Despite fierce fighting, the Canadians continued to penetrate into France after D-Day, helped by Allied airplanes. Throughout June and July of 1944, the fighting went on. At Caen, Canadian and British soldiers fought a German unit notorious for its cruelty but still captured the city. Canadian soldiers pushed on, and in August, they took the French town of Falaise. Soon, the Allies were chasing the Germans into Belgium and the Netherlands.

The Normandy Invasion was the largest invasion by sea in the world's history — more than three million troops took part. About 18 500 Canadians were killed or wounded during the three-month-long campaign that marked the beginning of the end for the German forces.

Scheldt Victory

Canadians moved along the Atlantic coast in late summer 1944, crushing German strongholds as they went. In early October 1944, they fought to gain control of the Scheldt River in Belgium. The ground was wet and swampy, and Canadian soldiers were often slogging through mud up to their waists.

It took a month of heavy fighting, but by November 8, the Canadians had taken over the Scheldt. This important victory allowed the Allies to send badly needed supplies up the river. But more than 6300 Canadians were killed or wounded as a result.

Conscription

Conscription became an issue in this world war as it had in the last (page 34). Prime Minister William Lyon Mackenzie King didn't want to make conscription law because it was unpopular and might cost him the next election. So in 1942, he held a vote to see whether Canadians would accept conscription. As in World War I, Quebec mostly voted no, while the rest of Canada mainly voted yes. But conscription was still too unpopular. King didn't introduce it until late in the war, in 1944.

1945 VE Day

The Allies kept advancing across Europe. Canadians helped push the Germans east through the Netherlands across the Rhine River, fighting across plains and through forests. British and American troops continued the advance, while Canadians were sent to the northern Netherlands.

Seeing his empire crumbling around him, Hitler committed suicide on April 30, 1945. Germany surrendered to the Allies. May 8 became known as VE Day — VE stands for "Victory in Europe."

Canadian troops liberated the Netherlands from German forces. The Canadian soldiers brought food, supplies and freedom to the cold, starving Dutch people. The war in Japan continued but would soon come to a sudden end. The United States now had devastating atomic bombs — made in part from Canadian uranium.

On August 6, a nuclear bomb was dropped on Hiroshima, one of Japan's major cities, then another on Nagasaki three days later. About 150 000 adults and children died within days or over the next year, while those who lived suffered from horrible radiation burns and sickness. Victory in Japan, or VJ Day, took place on August 14, 1945, when Japan surrendered. World War II was finally over.

During World War II, more than one million men and women joined Canada's armed forces.

Canadians served in Europe, the Mediterranean, the Middle East, North Africa, the Pacific and Southeast Asia. It was an incredible contribution by a country with a population of only 12 million.

At least 42 000 Canadians lost their lives during the war, and 55 000 were wounded. It was a high cost for Canada and its citizens, but an enemy as dangerous as Hitler had to be stopped. Canada's fighting forces gained great respect, from both their allies and enemies.

United Nations

For many years, countries had been looking for an organization to help solve arguments among them. Even before World War II ended, people had begun working to establish the United Nations (UN). In 1945, 50 countries, including Canada, joined to decide what the new organization would do. One of the UN's biggest roles is peacekeeping, and Canada has been very involved in this effort over the years (page 61).

The Holocaust

During World War II, more than six million Jewish people died at the hands of Adolf Hitler and his followers, the Nazis. He believed that Jews were an inferior race and should be eliminated.

Starting in 1940, Jews were sent to concentration camps, where they were tortured, starved, shot or gassed to death. When the war ended in Europe in May 1945, the death camps were liberated, and people discovered the horrific truth of how the Jews had been treated.

The surviving Jews again faced discrimination when they tried to leave Europe. Canada made it very difficult for them to immigrate to the country and accepted fewer than 5000 Jews, a far smaller number than similar nations. Many Canadians are still disturbed and embarrassed by the country's failure to help these desperate people.

1946 Viola Desmond stands for equality

When Viola Desmond's car broke down in New Glasgow, Nova Scotia, on November 8, 1946, she didn't know she was about to make history. Stuck in New Glasgow overnight, she bought a movie ticket and sat in the theatre's main-floor section. She didn't notice her ticket was for the balcony. Only white people could sit on the main floor. Black people had to sit upstairs.

When told to move, Viola tried to buy a ticket for the main floor. The teller refused. This was the last straw. Viola had put up with enough racial discrimination. She immediately returned to her seat on the main floor and sat there until a police officer carried her out.

The next day, Viola was charged with cheating the

province of Nova Scotia. The balcony-seat ticket that she'd bought was cheaper by one cent than the main-floor seat she'd sat in. Mention of skin colour was carefully avoided. Viola was found guilty.

Viola fought her conviction, and many people, including newspaper publisher Carrie Best (right), helped. Although she lost all of her appeals, Viola had the

courage to battle discrimination. Finally, in 1954, Nova Scotia outlawed racial segregation (separation due to race).

1947 Alberta oil

In 1947, oil was discovered at Leduc, south of Edmonton. This oil field and others found over the next 30 years made Alberta wealthy. Jobs were plentiful in the oil industry, and Edmonton and Calgary grew into large centres. Today, oil is one of Canada's top exports. It's now also extracted from Alberta's oil sands, or tar sands, which are a mixture of clay, sand, water and oil. While Canada's economy depends on this oil, the extraction process is controversial because it pollutes the air, land and water.

1948 *Refus global*

A group of artists and intellectuals in Quebec challenged traditional values in the province when it published *Refus global* ("Total Refusal") in 1948. The document, or manifesto, also encouraged the Québécois to look beyond the borders of their province and be more open to international thinking.

Well-known Quebec artists Paul-Émile Borduas and Jean Paul Riopelle helped write *Refus global*. They were members of a group of artists called Les Automatistes — they believed in drawing or painting "automatically" without judging whether their work had meaning or was pleasing to look at.

Although controversial, *Refus global* is considered an important part of Quebec history.

"We must insist on having our say — do what you will with us, but hear us you must."

— from *Refus global*

It challenged the traditional Québécois lifestyle, including the religious values of the Roman Catholic Church, which were very much a part of life in Quebec at the time.

The manifesto was one of the causes of the Quiet Revolution (page 67), a period of intense economic and social change in Quebec during the 1960s. *Refus global* also increased Quebec nationalism.

Some people in Quebec were so upset with the ideas included in *Refus global* that Paul-Émile lost his teaching job, and because of his views, he had trouble finding another one. But his writings and art changed how many Québécois saw themselves and their society.

1949 Oscar Peterson at Carnegie Hall

As a teenager in Montreal, Oscar Peterson found that playing piano was a great way to attract girls. Others took notice of his talent, too. He won a national music contest when he was just 14 and soon was playing jazz piano on radio shows broadcast across the country.

By 1948, Oscar's speedy fingers and musical sense had him playing with the best jazz musicians. In September 1949, he performed at Carnegie Hall in New York City as a surprise guest. Even though he wasn't the main attraction, he left the audience awestruck. It was a performance that would bring him international fame.

The Oscar Peterson Trio soon became known as the hardest-working group in jazz. One year,

the trio recorded 11 albums. Despite his success, Oscar had to deal with prejudice because of his skin colour.

In a career of more than 50 years, Oscar recorded lots of top-selling albums, gained millions

of fans and became a jazz composer. He received many awards for his music, including eight Grammy Awards and the Praemium Imperiale, an important international arts prize.

1950 Korean War begins

After World War II, Korea didn't have a government. It broke into two parts: North Korea, backed by China and the Soviet Union (now Russia), and South Korea, backed by the Americans. When North Koreans invaded the south on June 25, 1950, the United Nations (page 55) ordered them to get out. But the North Koreans refused to leave, so the United Nations decided to send in troops. The majority of these forces were American, but thousands of Canadians went as well. The first Canadian battalion arrived in Korea in December 1950.

Canadian soldiers fought North Korean troops, bravely defending strategic positions, even when they were vastly outnumbered. They patrolled hills and mountains, scouting out the enemy's position and ambushing enemy troops. During storms, patrols had to be careful not to be cut off from the rest of their unit.

Eight ships of the Royal Canadian Navy patrolled the coast of South Korea. A transport squadron of the Royal Canadian Air Force flew 600 round trips over the Pacific, carrying soldiers and supplies. Other Canadian pilots destroyed or damaged 20 North Korean jet fighters.

1951 Battle of Kapyong

On April 24, 1951, Canadian soldiers battled all night to hold back fierce attacks by Chinese forces in the Kapyong (now Gapyong) River Valley. This was an important route for moving troops. Wave after wave of attackers fought the Canadians with bayonets and in hand-to-hand combat in the hills surrounding the valley. It was some of the heaviest fighting the Canadians endured during the entire Korean War.

About 700 Canadians fought against 5000 enemy soldiers, preventing them from taking the Kapyong River Valley and stopping them from ultimately capturing Seoul, the capital of Korea. Canadians inflicted heavy casualties on the enemy: approximately 1000 Chinese soldiers were killed and 1000 were injured, compared to 10 Canadian soldiers killed and 23 wounded.

Today, the Battle of Kapyong is seen as one of Canada's greatest, but least-known, military achievements. Canadian soldiers won many awards for their bravery, including medals from the United States, which is a rare honour for Canadian fighters.

1952 Koje-Do

In May 1952, Canadians were called to the island of Koje-Do (now Geojedo), where huge compounds held 160 000 Chinese and North Korean prisoners of war. But these captured soldiers and officers had rebelled and taken over the American-operated camp. The American government called in Canadian troops to help recapture the camps.

A company of Canadians arrived in Koje-Do on May 25, 1952. Without causing any bloodshed, these soldiers helped the Americans restore order in the camp. Their main responsibility was to guard a compound of about 3200 prisoners, most of whom were North Korean officers.

The captives taunted their captors but the soldiers maintained control of the compound for six weeks. Finally, American soldiers and tanks rolled into the prison and were able to take over.

Even though the Canadian soldiers were successful, the Canadian government was upset that its soldiers had been sent to Koje-Do without its consent. It was the Canadian army's policy to keep its troops together and under its own country's command. Canada protested against the United States government to ensure that in the future, Canadian troops stay under Canadian command.

1953 Korean War ends

A ceasefire was finally negotiated, and the Korean War ended on July 27, 1953. Of the 26 791 Canadians who served in the war, 1042 were wounded and 516 were killed. Canada made a larger contribution in relation to its population than most other countries involved.

Sometimes the Korean War is called Canada's "forgotten war." It took place so soon after World War II that people didn't want to think about war again. As well, the Korean War ended in a stalemate, so there was no victory to celebrate. Canadian soldiers were heroes to the people they had liberated, but they felt no one back home cared.

It was many years before the Canadian government officially acknowledged the sacrifice of the Korean War soldiers. On July 27, 1997, in Brampton, Ontario, the Korean Veterans Wall of Remembrance was unveiled. This long, curving memorial wall includes the names of the Canadian soldiers who died in this war.

Korea continues to be divided between North Korea and South Korea. Troops from both sides still stand watch on either side of the zone that separates the two countries.

BOOM YEARS 1954–1966

By the mid-1950s, World War II had been over for 10 years, and Canada's future looked promising once again. Four million Canadian babies were born in the 1950s alone in what would become known as the baby boom.

Canada's economy was also booming, and people could afford more comfortable lifestyles than during the war years. Some people moved out of the cities to the suburbs, where they could buy larger homes. Most people now owned a car, so drive-in restaurants and movie theatres sprang up. Many Canadian homes had their first television, and that changed how families spent time together.

New technologies helped improve transportation, and the country's first subway was running in Toronto by 1954. The St. Lawrence Seaway opened in 1959. Its canals and locks allowed large ships to sail far inland from the Atlantic Ocean. On July 30, 1962, the Trans-Canada Highway officially opened.

But not everyone in Canada was enjoying boom years. Strikes and labour unrest showed that workers wanted change. People's rights, especially the rights of Aboriginal peoples, black Canadians, immigrants and women, also came to the forefront in the 1960s.

1954 Marilyn Bell's swim

For years, people had tried to swim across Lake Ontario, but failed. In 1954, American swimmer Florence Chadwick was promised $10 000 (worth about $87 000 today) if she completed the swim. Some Torontonians thought Canadians should be involved, too, so Marilyn Bell and Winnie Roach-Leuszler (the first Canadian to swim the English Channel) agreed to swim.

The swimmers had to wait for the best weather and water conditions. Just before midnight on September 8, the time seemed right. The late hour had made Marilyn sleepy, but diving into the frigid water at Youngstown, New York, jolted her awake!

The 16-year-old battled high waves, lamprey eels and oil spills. The other two much more experienced swimmers gave up,

but Marilyn swam on, at times barely conscious. When she finally reached Toronto almost 21 hours later, she and her coach were shocked to see huge crowds on shore cheering for her.

Marilyn had been motivated by Winnie's success at swimming the English Channel. In turn, Marilyn inspired Vicki Keith, who swam across all five Great Lakes

in 1988, and 14-year-old Trinity Arsenault, who in 2014 became the youngest person to swim across Lake Ontario.

"I did it for Canada."

— Marilyn Bell

1955 Fans riot over Maurice Richard

Maurice Richard was one of the top players in the National Hockey League (NHL). He was nicknamed the "Rocket" because of his speed on the ice. One of the highest scorers and most intense players in NHL history, he terrified his opponents. He was captain of the Montreal Canadiens, and his message to his teammates before every game was, "Let's go out and win it."

The Rocket was so passionate about hockey that he often lost his temper. On March 13, 1955, he attacked another player and punched a linesman. He was suspended for the rest of the season, as well as for all of the play-offs. His fans were furious — they knew this would likely mean he wouldn't win his first point-scoring title and it would cost the Canadiens the Stanley Cup.

On March 17, 1955, the Canadiens' supporters took to the streets of Montreal in one of the worst riots in Canadian history. People were injured, windows were smashed and stores were looted. Not only did the riot show how loyal the Rocket's fans were, but it also demonstrated how passionately people felt about the Montreal Canadiens and their Québécois identity.

The next year, the Rocket led the Canadiens to a Stanley Cup win. During his career, he played on eight Stanley Cup–winning teams and was also the first player to score 50 goals in 50 games.

Did You Know?

The Maurice Richard Trophy is awarded each year to the NHL's top goal scorer.

1956 Suez crisis

When Egypt suddenly took over the Suez Canal in 1956, many countries worried they were on the brink of war. The canal was located in Egypt, but it was run by a French and British company. The company wanted to take back control of the canal. Egypt refused, and on October 31, Britain and France invaded the area.

Lester B. Pearson, the secretary of state for external affairs, suggested to the United Nations (page 55) that it create an emergency force to supervise a ceasefire between the two sides. His idea led to the first international peacekeeping unit, under the command of another Canadian, General E. L. M. Burns.

The following year, Lester won the Nobel Peace Prize (page 40), one of the world's highest honours. He is the only Canadian ever to win this prize. In 1963, he became Canada's prime minister.

The Suez crisis reminded Canada and the world that countries needed to work together for peace. In 1949, Canada had become a member of the North Atlantic Treaty Organization (NATO), a group of 10 European countries plus the United States, which promised to work together if any of their countries were attacked. (There are now 28 countries in NATO.)

In 1958, Canada joined the United States to create the North American Air Defense Command (NORAD). Today, it uses aircraft, radar and satellites to watch for activity in the skies over North America.

Did You Know?

August 9 is Peacekeepers' Day in Canada, which honours Canadians who help maintain peace. The day was chosen because on that date in 1974, nine Canadian peacekeepers were killed in Syria.

1957 Canada Council for the Arts

By the middle of the century, Canadian culture was coming into its own. In 1949, the federal government asked a team led by Vincent Massey to investigate the state of the arts in Canada. The Massey Commission, as it would become known, published its report in 1951.

One of its main suggestions was that the government should provide funding for the arts, and the Canada Council for the Arts was created in 1957. The Canada Council gives out grants and awards, including the Governor General's Awards — one of the country's top honours.

Many arts institutions were established during these years. The National Ballet of Canada was formed in 1951, the Stratford Festival and the National Library of Canada (now Library and Archives Canada) opened in 1953, and in 1957 the Comédie-Canadienne was formed by the actor and playwright Gratien Gélinas. Meanwhile, the National Film Board, formed just before World War II, began to make dramas as well as its usual documentary films.

Canadian painting also flourished during this time. The Painters Eleven, a group of artists who painted in a more modern and abstract style than the Group of Seven, held their first exhibition in 1954. Just two years earlier, Canada participated for the first time in the Venice Biennale, an important international art exhibition held in Italy.

Some of Canada's most beloved writers, such as Mavis Gallant, Margaret Laurence (below), Leonard Cohen (page 91) and Mordecai Richler (page 93), published their first books during these years.

Margaret Laurence

At age seven, Jean Margaret Wemyss began writing. She continued to write throughout school, but it wasn't until she married John Laurence and moved to Africa in 1950 that she began to write seriously. When the family returned to Canada in 1957, she focused on writing about her own country.

Five of Margaret's most famous books take place in Manawaka, Manitoba, a made-up town based on her hometown of Neepawa. Of these, *A Jest of God* (1966) and *The Diviners* (1974) won the Governor General's Literary Awards. These books look at life in a small prairie town, as well as the conflict between fitting into society and being an individual. Margaret also wrote four books for children.

A good ear for dialogue and sensitivity to those cut off from society are two of the things that make Margaret's writing so powerful. She used her fame to advocate for environmental causes, peace and literacy.

1958 First Aboriginal senator

In 1958, James Gladstone, from the Blood Reserve in Alberta, became the first Status Indian appointed to the Senate of Canada. Ironically, he did not have the right to vote in federal elections until 1960 (see below) or in his home province of Alberta until 1965 because of his Aboriginal status. He was a strong champion of Aboriginal rights.

1959 Jacques Plante's goalie mask

When he was injured in a professional hockey game in November 1959, goalie Jacques Plante refused to return to the ice unless his coach allowed him to wear a mask. At that time, goalies in the National Hockey League (NHL) didn't wear them and often got hit in the face with pucks. Jacques wore his mask, his team won the game and soon many goalies imitated him.

The pride of the Montreal Canadiens, Jacques was an innovator in other ways, too. He was the first goalie to come out of his net to pass the puck up the ice to a teammate or to slip behind the goal and shoot the puck to a defenceman.

Jacques won the NHL's best-goalie award a record seven times and played on six Stanley Cup–winning teams. He is still one of the few goalies ever to win the NHL's trophy for most valuable player.

1960 Canadian Bill of Rights

In his first election campaign as Progressive Conservative Party leader, John Diefenbaker had promised Canadians new roads, towns and mining jobs in the North, more help for farmers and better programs for those in need. He also promised a bill of rights that would protect such basic human rights as freedom of speech and religion.

John's proudest achievement came in 1960 when Parliament passed the Canadian Bill of Rights. As well, he gave all Aboriginal Canadians the same right to vote and to own property as other Canadians.

In 1957, he appointed Ellen Fairclough (page 64) as the first female Cabinet minister (a member of Parliament who works closely with the prime minister). In 1958, he appointed James Gladstone (above) as the first Status Indian to the Senate.

In 1961, he led the move to stop trade with South Africa until it ended its racist policies.

To encourage Canadians to think about human rights, the Canadian Museum for Human Rights (below) opened in 2014. It's located in Winnipeg, Manitoba. Many diverse communities live there, including Aboriginal peoples, French speakers, Métis and others. The museum promotes respect for all and encourages people — and especially students — to think about human rights.

"Parliament is the place where your freedom and mine is maintained and preserved."

— John Diefenbaker

1961 New Democratic Party

Since 1932, the Co-operative Commonwealth Federation (CCF) had been a political party that appealed especially to farmers and workers. Its aims were economic cooperation and political reform, particularly to help Canadians affected by the Great Depression.

Some people in the CCF believed war was wrong, and this position was very unpopular with many Canadians during World War II. So the CCF decided to join with the Canadian Labour Congress to form a new party. In 1961, the New Democratic Party (NDP) was created.

Thomas "Tommy" Douglas became the new party's first leader and he would improve life for Canadians in many ways (page 65).

1962 Immigration laws change

In the 1800s and early 1900s, millions of people came to live in Canada, most from European countries. However, many faced prejudice and difficulties. For instance, Irish immigrants (page 9) fleeing the potato famine were often treated badly in Canada, and Chinese citizens had to pay an expensive tax to enter the country (page 16). Other nationalities and religious groups were also discriminated against.

On January 19, 1962, Canada's minister of citizenship and immigration, Ellen Fairclough (below), introduced a new act. Its purpose was to eliminate the discrimination that many newcomers faced when trying to come to Canada. The act said that any immigrant who didn't have a sponsor (someone to support them) but had the required education, skill or other qualification could live in Canada. They couldn't be discriminated against based on race, colour or nationality.

Newcomers to Canada from all countries were finally treated equally. Immigration increased quickly, especially from Asian and Caribbean (page 69) countries. Soon, more than half of Canada's immigrants came from countries outside Europe.

PROFILE

Ellen Fairclough

As minister of citizenship and immigration, Ellen Fairclough brought in regulations in 1962 to stop discrimination against immigrants based on their colour, race or home country. She was also responsible for responding to Aboriginal peoples' concerns, and two years earlier had gotten legislation passed giving them the vote in federal elections.

When Ellen entered politics in 1945, she joined the race for city council in Hamilton, Ontario — and lost by three votes. "No one can ever tell me," she said, "that a single vote does not count!"

In 1957, Ellen was the first woman appointed to the Cabinet. When Prime Minister John Diefenbaker went travelling in 1958, he made Ellen the acting prime minister of Canada. Although she held the position for less than two days, it signalled women's growing role in politics. Throughout her career, Ellen encouraged women to take part in politics and pushed for women to receive the same opportunities and pay as men.

1963 Gordie Howe's record

For five games, hockey star Gordon "Gordie" Howe had been kept off the scoreboard. The game on November 10, 1963, started the same way. Then, with the second period almost over, Gordie took a pass and drilled a blistering shot at the Montreal Canadiens' net. Score!

It was Gordie's 545th goal and it made him the National Hockey League's (NHL's) all-time leading scorer. He would hold the record for almost 30 years. Thanks to his puck handling, speed, smarts and toughness, Gordie was one of the top-five scorers in the NHL for 20 straight seasons — few players even last that long!

1964 "The medium is the message"

Marshall McLuhan was a university professor and philosopher who was interested in technology and communication. He wrote about how the invention of the printing press changed the world hundreds of years ago, and how mass media (television, radio, newspapers, advertising) affected people of his day.

In 1964, Marshall published the famous statement "The medium is the message," meaning that how a message is delivered is part of the message itself. Through his books, Marshall changed the way people thought about technology and how it impacts their lives.

1965 Maple Leaf flag

In 1963, Prime Minister Lester B. Pearson (page 61) promised voters a new, distinctively Canadian flag. He was met with furious opposition from Conservative leader John Diefenbaker (page 63) and from Canadians who saw a new flag as a rejection of the country's British roots. Until then, the Canadian flag had been the Red Ensign, which included the Union Jack (Great Britain's flag) in its design.

After months of bitter debate, the flag bill was finally passed in December 1964. On February 15, 1965, the new Maple Leaf flag flew for the first time over Parliament Hill.

1966 Medicare

When Canadians are sick or hurt, they can go to the doctor or hospital without having to pay. That's because with universal health care (or "medicare"), doctors are paid by the government.

Universal health care came into effect under the Medical Care Act in 1966 thanks to Tommy Douglas, who is known as the Father of Medicare. In 1911, seven-year-old Tommy had bone disease in one leg. His parents couldn't afford the surgery to save it, so Tommy faced amputation. His leg was spared when a doctor offered to operate for free. Tommy later vowed to make sure that poverty would never stop people from getting medical care.

The Great Depression (page 47) hit the people of Saskatchewan, where Tommy lived, especially hard. He decided the way to make change was to get into politics. Because he was a spellbinding and witty speaker, people listened and, in 1935, elected him as a member of Canada's federal Parliament. Tommy switched to provincial politics in 1944 and was elected premier of Saskatchewan.

In 1961, Tommy returned to federal politics and became the first leader of the New Democratic Party (page 64).

HAPPY BIRTHDAY! 1967–1979

Canadians looked forward to their country's 100th birthday with excitement and optimism. Expo 67 in Montreal was the most successful World's Fair yet. For the first time, many people around the world began to notice what a great country Canada was.

Centennial projects sprang up across the nation, including new community centres, art galleries and parks that people still enjoy. Quality of life and prosperity were at an all-time high in Canada.

Canada began to influence the arts scene around the world in the late 1960s and 1970s. Singers such as Leonard Cohen (page 91), Joni Mitchell (page 92) and Neil Young, and the Winnipeg band The Guess Who, were becoming well known. Writer Alice Munro (page 87) published her first collection of short stories in 1968, while Margaret Atwood's (page 82) first novel was released in 1969.

Canadians were more proud of their country than ever before as it entered its second century.

1967 Canada celebrates!

On July 1, 1967, Canada turned 100 years old, and Canadians celebrated all year with parties, competitions and exhibitions. The greatest celebration was Expo 67, the World's Fair held in Montreal from April 27 to October 29. It attracted more than 50 million visitors. The fair had pavilions from all over the world that highlighted the theme Man and His World. Another attraction was Habitat 67, a futuristic-looking housing project where people still live today.

As Canadians welcomed visitors from around the world, they felt immensely proud of all that their country had achieved in the past century.

To continue celebrating the country's achievements, the Order of Canada was established to honour great Canadians. The first members were inducted on July 1, 1967, and included an opera singer, an author, a doctor and a hockey player.

1968 Parti Québécois

The 1960s saw a surge of nationalism in Quebec — a pride in being Québécois. Poets, novelists, filmmakers and other artists celebrated Quebec's culture and history in their works. For instance, when Gilles Vigneault wrote the song "Mon pays" ("My Country"), he meant Quebec, not Canada.

This nationalism was largely inspired by the changes made by Premier Jean Lesage and his Liberal government from 1960 to 1966. They set out to make Quebec more up-to-date — and more Quebec-owned. For example, they took over many privately owned electric-power companies. They also put education firmly under government control and reorganized it, providing more higher education, especially in the sciences. This dramatic shift in events in Quebec would become known as the Quiet Revolution.

More and more Québécois thought of their province as a distinct nation, and some wanted it to become a separate country. Others wanted it to remain part of Canada but to increase the use of French in Quebec.

In 1968, René Lévesque and others founded a provincial political party called Parti Québécois. Its aim was to make Quebec a separate nation while still sharing Canada's money system, among other things. This proposed arrangement was called sovereignty-association.

René became premier of Quebec in 1976, and a year later, his government passed a controversial law (Bill 101) to preserve French language and culture in Quebec. This law stated that all children had to attend French schools (except if their parents had gone to English schools in Quebec) and that all signs had to be in French. While parts of Bill 101 have since been changed, the language debate in Quebec continues.

1969 Official Languages Act

The growing unrest in Quebec during the 1960s (above) led to the Royal Commission on Bilingualism and Biculturalism. From 1963 to 1969, this delegation looked at the state of French and English languages in Canada.

One of the outcomes was the Official Languages Act, which was passed by Pierre Trudeau's government in 1969. The act said that both French and English must be available to people in Canada's courts and all other branches of the federal government. Most French Canadians working in federal jobs were already bilingual, but most English Canadians were not, and many didn't want to learn French.

New Brunswick made English and French official languages in 1969. In all other provinces, except Quebec, English is the official language.

1970 October Crisis

In the 1960s, some people wanted Quebec to be independent from Canada (page 67). Among them was a group called the Front de libération du Québec (FLQ), which began setting off bombs in Montreal. Their terrorist actions killed 6 people and injured at least 40.

When the FLQ kidnapped British diplomat James Cross and Quebec politician Pierre Laporte in October 1970, Canadians were outraged. Prime Minister Pierre Trudeau sent in armed troops to help the police. He also used the War Measures Act to extend the power of the government and give police the right to arrest people without explanation.

The October Crisis was the first time the act had been used in peacetime, and some Canadians thought using it was going too far. The members of the FLQ were eventually captured, but not before murdering Pierre Laporte.

1971 CANDU reactor

As the country needed more energy to power its growing population, a Canadian nuclear power company began developing nuclear reactors to generate electricity.

In 1971, the first CANDU reactor began operation in Pickering, Ontario. The name is short for Canada Deuterium Uranium reactor. Deuterium is another name for "heavy water," or water with a slightly different chemistry. Nuclear reactions heat the heavy water, which boils regular water and makes steam to power turbines. That creates electricity.

The CANDU reactor produced more electricity than any other nuclear power operation at the time. The technology is used around the world, including in Argentina, China and Pakistan.

1972 CN Tower

When Toronto's skyscrapers increased in number and height through the 1960s, they lowered the quality of television and radio broadcast signals in the area. The CN Tower was built by the Canadian National Railway Company to improve communications.

Work began in 1972 and the CN Tower was completed in 1976. At that point, the tower was the tallest freestanding structure in the world, a title it held for more than 30 years. It still boasts the record for the world's highest and largest revolving restaurant, as well as the longest metal staircase in the world!

1973 Caribbean immigration

Immigration from the Caribbean (including such countries as Barbados, Haiti, Jamaica and Trinidad) began to swell in the 1960s. That's because Canada's immigration laws changed in 1962 (page 64). By 1973, people from the Caribbean made up almost 13 percent of all Canada's immigrants.

Most English-speaking immigrants from the Caribbean started their new life in Ontario. People from Haiti, many of whom spoke French, tended to move to Quebec, especially Montreal. All of the immigrants from the Caribbean came to Canada for jobs, and they provided much-needed skilled labour.

Caribana

The Caribana festival (now called the Scotiabank Toronto Caribbean Carnival) is a celebration of Caribbean culture. It began in 1967 in Toronto to celebrate Canada's 100th birthday. That year, the festival was just a short parade. Today, this festival is North America's largest cultural celebration, spread over three weeks in July and August. The parade, with its amazing costumes, is still the festival's highlight. But Caribana also includes shows, competitions, dances and even a junior carnival just for kids.

1974 First female lieutenant-governor

Pauline McGibbon always said that she owed her appointment as lieutenant-governor to the women who fought hard for their rights. When she was given the position in 1974, Pauline was not only the first female lieutenant-governor in Ontario, but also in all of Canada.

Each province and territory has a lieutenant-governor (in the territories, they are called commissioners) who represents Canada's monarch (the king or queen of Britain). Lieutenant-governors attend events and ceremonies and give royal assent to bills passed in their provinces, turning these bills into laws.

Pauline was known for her sense of humour and love of people. She worked all her life doing volunteer work to make her community a better place. The arts in Ontario were her particular focus. Pauline changed the job of lieutenant-governor by travelling throughout the province and meeting with many ordinary Ontarians. She also opened her official office to thousands of visitors and held many receptions.

Education was also very important to Pauline. With dedication, warmth and determination, she changed how people saw the position of lieutenant-governor and made it much more accessible to all Ontarians.

Other lieutenant-governors have made headlines with their firsts, too. Ralph Steinhauer of Alberta was appointed Canada's first Aboriginal lieutenant-governor in 1974. Canada's first black lieutenant-governor was Lincoln Alexander, appointed to the position in Ontario in 1985.

PROFILE

Jeanne Sauvé

The Governor General represents Canada's monarch for the entire country, just as lieutenant-governors represent the monarch in the provinces. Jeanne-Mathilde Sauvé became Canada's first female Governor General in 1984, which she said was "a magnificent breakthrough for women."

But it wasn't the only first in Jeanne's life. In 1972, she had become the first Quebec woman appointed to the federal Cabinet. And in 1980, she'd been made the first female Speaker of the House of Commons, keeping order in the house and managing staff and expenses.

1975 Beaver becomes official emblem

One of Canada's first important industries, the fur trade, was based on the beaver. When European settlers arrived in the 1600s, they traded with Aboriginal people for local resources — including beaver pelts. At the time, hats made of beaver fur were very fashionable in Europe and in high demand. To recognize the historic fur trade, Canada made the beaver an official emblem in 1975. In 2017, Canada designated an official bird for the country.

Did You Know?

The maple leaf has long been a Canadian symbol, but it wasn't until 1996 that the maple tree became the country's official arboreal (tree) emblem.

1976 Montreal Olympic Games

Let the Games begin! In July and August 1976, Montreal became the first and, so far, only Canadian city to host the Summer Olympic Games. Hosting the games required building a stadium, and French architect Roger Taillibert was the person for the job. To this day, the Olympic Stadium remains a unique landmark in the Montreal skyline.

Canada has hosted the Winter Olympics twice, first in Calgary in 1988 and again in Vancouver in 2010.

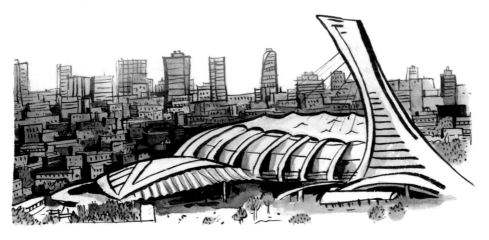

Arctic Winter Games

The people who live at the top of the world enjoy getting together to celebrate life in the North. One of their favourite events is the Arctic Winter Games. Held every two years in a different arctic community, these games are the "Olympics of the North."

Through the long, dark winter, young athletes practice traditional Inuit sports, such as the high kick, arm pull and knuckle hop. Drummers, throat-singers and dancers also spend the winter practicing for their parts in the games' opening and closing ceremonies.

In March, when daylight is returning, the games are a welcome break from winter, although spring may still be months away. Winners take home *ulu*-shaped medals, modeled after the knife traditionally used by Inuit people.

FIRST

Now considered one of the world's top film festivals, the Toronto International Film Festival (TIFF) was first held in 1976. Then called the Festival of Festivals, it had trouble getting big Hollywood studios to show their movies.

Today, many well-known movies have premiered at TIFF. More than 400 000 people attend each year and about 400 movies are shown. Movies that are successful at this festival often go on to win Academy Awards, the top movie prize.

TIFF brings Hollywood glamour and movie stars to Toronto and also helps celebrate Canadian cinema and talent, such as directors David Cronenberg, Atom Egoyan (page 91) and Sarah Polley (page 93). The festival is also known for showcasing movies from Africa, Asia and South America.

1977 First Inuk senator

Inuit Canadians were granted the vote in federal elections in 1950, but it wasn't until 1977 that an Inuk (the singular form of Inuit) would sit in Parliament.

Willie Adams was born in Kuujjuak (then called Fort Chimo), Quebec, in 1934. He later moved to Rankin Inlet, Nunavut, where he became an electrician and businessperson. Willie served on a local council, and then in 1970, he was elected a member of the Northwest Territories Council (now the Legislative Assembly of the Northwest Territories).

Because of his work as a northern politician, Willie was appointed to the Senate in 1977. He was proud to be the first Inuk to hold this position. As a member of Senate committees, he dealt with such topics as fisheries, natural resources and transportation.

Willie was always especially concerned with issues that affected Inuit people and worked hard to protect their rights. He was a member of the Senate until 2009, making him one of Canada's longest-serving senators.

There have been many other Inuk firsts in Canadian politics. In 1979, Peter Ittinuar from the Northwest Territories became the first Inuk elected as a Member of Parliament to the House of Commons. The first female Inuk premier was Nellie Cournoyea (page 78), who led the Northwest Territories from 1991 to 1995. In 2008, Leona Aglukkaq became the first Inuk appointed to the federal Cabinet.

1978 Wayne Gretzky goes pro

No wonder he's been called "The Great One" ever since he was a kid. When he was 10, Wayne Gretzky scored 378 goals in just 68 hockey games. In 1978, when he was just 17 years old, he was the youngest player in professional sports in North America.

When Wayne played for the National Hockey League's (NHL's) Edmonton Oilers during the 1985–1986 season, he scored a record 215 points. He has set or tied 61 NHL records and is the league's all-time leading scorer, with 2857 points. Wayne is the only player to have reached 2000 career points.

Wayne began playing hockey on a rink his dad had made by flooding their backyard in Brantford, Ontario. He credits his father for encouraging him without pushing too hard. Wayne would practice for hours — he loved it so much that it never seemed like work. In the NHL, he would exhaust his teammates with his long practices.

Wayne wasn't big, and his style wasn't smooth, but he had an accurate shot and an incredible instinct for the game. He seemed to see plays happen in slow motion and so could anticipate where the puck was heading. Players called the area behind the net "Gretzky's office," because that's where he liked to set up plays. And Wayne had the greatest pass in hockey history — his record number of 1963 assists proves it.

Although proud of his hockey records, Wayne is more pleased that he has raised hockey's profile around the world. He was executive director of Canada's men's Olympic hockey team in 2002 and led them to the gold medal.

1979 David Suzuki on television

David Suzuki is an award-winning scientist, environmentalist, writer and TV host. David first became famous for his work in genetics, the study of heredity. In 1979, he began hosting *The Nature of Things*, one of the most successful television shows in Canadian history. By explaining science in an  interesting way, David has changed the way Canadians understand science and has helped to raise awareness of environmental issues around the world.

THE DIGITAL AGE 1980–1999

Before the 1980s, some businesses had computers, but few people had them at home. By the end of the millennium, many families had a home computer. Soon, the internet would revolutionize how people communicated.

Most homes had cable television, which gave people access to many new channels. Beginning in 1984, Canadians watched MuchMusic for the latest music videos. People could easily rent or record TV shows and movies with videocassette recorder (VCR) technology. But technology was quickly evolving, and by the end of the 1990s, a new format — DVD (digital video discs) — was already popular.

Technology wasn't the only thing changing by the 1990s. Global warming became a major concern as weather patterns shifted and the environment heated up. Many Canadians started to worry about how to reduce pollution and keep their environment safe.

1980 Terry Fox's run

When Terrance "Terry" Fox was only 18 years old, he discovered he had a rare form of bone cancer. His right leg had to be amputated above the knee. Terry became determined to do something so that other people wouldn't have to go through the same thing. He decided to run across Canada to raise money for cancer research and increase awareness of the disease. Terry called his run the Marathon of Hope.

On April 12, 1980, Terry began his incredible journey in St. John's, Newfoundland. He ran a distance equal to a marathon every day. He faced icy storms, blustery winds and burning heat, and he still kept running.

But on September 1, 1980, Terry's run ended in Thunder Bay, Ontario — the cancer had spread to his lungs, forcing him to stop. He died less than a year later.

"I just wish people would realize that anything is possible if you try," Terry once said. This Canadian hero realized his dream of raising the equivalent of one dollar from every Canadian. His Marathon of Hope united the country behind him and made Canada proud.

Today, the Terry Fox Foundation continues his dream of fundraising to find a cure for cancer. The Terry Fox Run is held each year across Canada and around the world. It has become one of the largest single-day fundraising events for cancer, all thanks to one courageous hero who had a dream.

"Dreams are made if people only try. I believe in miracles ... I have to ... because somewhere the hurting must stop."
— Terry Fox

1981 Canadarm

It was only 15 m (50 ft.) long, but the Canadarm cost $110 million to build! This six-jointed arm and hand was created by a team of Canadian engineers and used by NASA for 30 years to grab and manoeuvre objects — such as satellites and even astronauts — in space with amazing precision. First used on the space shuttle *Columbia* in November 1981, the Canadarm put Canada at the forefront of space robotics.

1982 Canadian Charter of Rights and Freedoms

When Pierre Trudeau was re-elected as prime minister in 1980, he was determined to "bring the constitution home." The constitution was the British North America (BNA) Act, which had founded Canada in 1867 and provided the rules and principles to govern the country. Because it was a British act, any changes to it that Canada wanted had to be made by the British Parliament. In the past, Canadian politicians had often tried to write a new Canadian constitution. But they could never agree on the rules

governing how changes would be made to it.

For more than a year, Pierre negotiated with the premiers of the provinces, trying to get them to agree on the details of the new act. Eventually, all provinces

"A country is something that is built every day out of certain basic values."

— Pierre Trudeau

except Quebec agreed, and the Constitution Act was signed by Queen Elizabeth during her visit to Canada in 1982. The act allowed changes to the constitution to be made in Canada, and included the Canadian Charter of Rights and Freedoms, which states that all people are equal before the law, whatever their race, religion, sex, age or mental or physical ability. The Charter guarantees Aboriginal rights and supports "the multicultural heritage of Canadians."

1983 Céline Dion's gold record

Céline Dion recorded a demo tape in 1980 when she was only 12 years old. She sent it to René Angélil, a Quebec record producer and manager, who was amazed by her voice. René believed in Céline's talent so much that he mortgaged his house to pay for the recording of her first album. He later became her husband.

In 1983, Céline became the first Canadian to earn a gold record in France for her album *Les chemins de ma maison (The Paths of My House)*. Her album *Let's Talk About Love*, which included the song "My Heart Will Go On" from the movie *Titanic*, was number one around the world and set a record in Canada for copies sold in its first week.

Céline has sold more than 200 million albums in her career, making her one of the most successful pop singers ever.

1984 First Canadian in space

Marc Garneau never dreamed of being an astronaut because he thought Canadians would never have the chance to explore space. That changed in 1983 when he saw an advertisement saying that Canada was looking for astronauts. Marc was one of the lucky six picked from more than 4000 applicants. After a few months of training, his career was launched.

In October 1984, aboard the space shuttle *Challenger*, this quiet, careful engineer became the first Canadian in space. Marc

> *"I've fulfilled just about all of the things that I would have ever dreamed — even many that I didn't even dream that I could ever do."*
>
> — Marc Garneau

took a hockey stick and puck with him to represent his country.

In May 1996, Marc rocketed into space again, this time on the *Endeavour*. He used the Canadarm (page 73) to retrieve a satellite and carried out experiments, including two designed by Canadian kids. He returned to space again in December 2000 to help build the International Space Station. With this flight, Marc became the first Canadian to fly three missions in space.

Marc was the president of the Canadian Space Agency (page 77) from 2001 to 2006. He then became a Member of Parliament, with a special interest in foreign affairs, defence issues and natural resources. In 2015, he was named minister of transport in Justin Trudeau's Liberal government.

Did You Know?

Roberta Bondar was Canada's first female astronaut. Her mission aboard the *Discovery* took place from January 22 to 30, 1992.

1985 Rick Hansen's world tour

Richard "Rick" Hansen was a high-energy kid who loved sports. But a truck accident severed his spinal cord and left his legs paralyzed when he was just 15. Scared and in a lot of pain, Rick was still determined not to give up sports. Within a few years, he had become a world-class wheelchair athlete.

Rick's friend Terry Fox (page 72) inspired him to raise money for spinal-cord research and wheelchair sports. Rick decided to do it by wheelchairing 40 000 km (24 855 mi.) — a distance equal to once around the world. His Man in Motion World Tour left Vancouver in March 1985 and eventually took him across 34 countries.

Rick was on the road for more than two years, wheeling 50 to 70 km (31 to 43 mi.) daily. His travels took him through mountains, deserts and blinding snowstorms. When it was over, the Man in Motion tour had raised $26 million.

Rick continues to promote both spinal-cord research and disabled athletes through his Rick Hansen Institute.

1986 Great books for kids!

Until the 1970s, most books that Canadian kids read were from Britain, France or the United States. Then in the early 1970s, publishing houses in Canada started making children's books that were written and illustrated by Canadians.

These great stories not only tell young readers about the world, but also tell the world what is important to Canadians.

When kids first read the picture book *Franklin in the Dark* in 1986, they immediately fell in love with Franklin, a turtle who is brave and full of mischief. This book, written by Paulette Bourgeois and illustrated by Brenda Clark, was the first in a long series that has sold more than 60 million copies around the world, been translated into about 40 languages and turned into two television series.

That same year, Robert Munsch published his now classic picture book *Love You Forever*, illustrated by Sheila McGraw. Many people thought the story was too serious for kids — but they were wrong! It would become one of the bestselling children's books of all time.

1987 Meech Lake Accord

The Constitution Act of 1982 (page 73) was enacted without Quebec's consent. Hoping to gain the province's support, Prime Minister Brian Mulroney met with the premiers of the 10 provinces at Meech Lake, near Ottawa, in 1987. After much discussion, they signed an accord (an official agreement) that declared Quebec a "distinct society" and gave it and other provinces some new powers. But many Canadians disliked the accord. Some thought it gave the provinces too much power. Others said it favoured Quebec. When the accord was put before the provincial legislatures, it didn't get approval in Manitoba and Newfoundland.

Elijah Harper, an Aboriginal member of the Manitoba legislature, blocked the Meech Lake Accord by refusing to agree to it. One reason he refused was because the accord gave the provinces the right to prevent the Yukon Territory and Northwest Territories (where many Aboriginal people live) from ever becoming provinces.

Brian Mulroney tried again with the Charlottetown Accord in 1992. This time, he met with Aboriginal leaders and the leaders of the two territories as well as the premiers. But when it was put to a vote in a public referendum, Canadians, including most Québécois, voted against it.

The Canadian Loonie

The loonie, or one-dollar coin, replaced the one-dollar bill in 1987. The coin is nicknamed for the loon on its front side.

A loonie was hidden in the ice hockey rink at the 2002 Winter Olympic Games, and Canada's men's and women's hockey teams both won gold! In 1996, the two-dollar coin, or toonie, was introduced, while in 2012, Canada's last penny was minted.

1988 First Aboriginal woman in Parliament

In 1988, Ethel Blondin-Andrew became the first Aboriginal woman to be elected to the House of Commons.

Born in Tulita, Northwest Territories, Ethel was a member of the Dene First Nation and a strong advocate for Aboriginal peoples during her time in office. As the minister of state for children and youth, she also worked on issues affecting young people, especially youth employment. She paved the way for other Aboriginal women in Parliament.

1989 Canadian Space Agency

In the 1980s, Canada was making a lot of progress in the space sciences. To continue developing the field, the Canadian Space Agency (CSA) was created on December 14, 1989. This organization promotes the peaceful use of space for the benefit of all Canadians. Its work includes managing the Canadian Astronaut Program. The CSA helped train such astronauts as Marc Garneau (page 74), Roberta Bondar (page 74) and Chris Hadfield (page 91). The agency also funded Canadarm2, the successor to the Canadarm (page 73), as well as Dextre, a robotic hand on the International Space Station.

One of the most important parts of the CSA is its satellite program. RADARSAT, a remote sensing satellite that was developed by both Canada and the United States, was launched in 1995. It uses advanced microwave technology to provide high-resolution images of Earth, no matter how cloudy, dark or foggy the weather. RADARSAT can monitor natural resources and inspect the environment.

The CSA also works with other countries, including Japan and Russia, on projects such as the International Space Station. In this way, it helps to promote international cooperation through scientific research.

The Montreal Massacre

On December 6, 1989, 14 women at Montreal's École Polytechnique were shot and killed. The incident has become known as the Montreal Massacre. The gunman felt that feminists had ruined his life and that women shouldn't be studying to become engineers at the school.

Since this sad day, Canadians have marked December 6 as the National Day of Remembrance and Action on Violence Against Women. Men and women across the country gather to remember the women who died in Montreal, as well as other women who have been the target of violence and discrimination.

1990 Oka Crisis

When the town of Oka, near Montreal, decided to build on land that had traditionally been used by the Mohawk — including a burial ground — a major controversy erupted.

Canada's army was called in when Mohawks of the Kanesatke reserve barricaded woods that were scheduled to be cut down to make way for an expanded golf course and a condominium development. Supporters from across the country joined in the protest. The standoff between soldiers, police and protesters lasted for more than two months in 1990, and before it ended, a police officer was killed.

The city's plans were eventually cancelled, and the Canadian government purchased the land to protect it from future development.

1991 Gulf War under way

For a long time, the Middle Eastern country of Iraq had felt its neighbour Kuwait was really part of Iraq. So in August 1990, Iraq invaded Kuwait. Canada was one

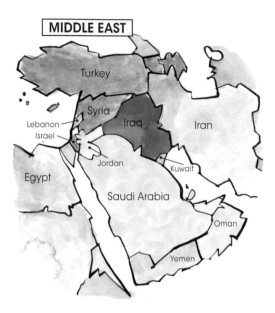

MIDDLE EAST

of the first countries to condemn the attack. The United Nations (page 55) ruled Iraq's actions were wrong and authorized the use of force to drive out the Iraqi soldiers. This conflict became known as the Gulf War.

Beginning in late 1990, 35 countries, including Canada, sent in troops to liberate Kuwait. In January 1991, an air war began. About 4000 Canadian Armed Forces personnel served in the region. The Gulf War marked the first time female Canadian soldiers took part in combat.

Canadian destroyers intercepted suspicious shipping in the area. In the air, Canadian

jet pilots attacked targets below, while other Canadian planes transported soldiers and cargo. On the ground, Canadian soldiers guarded the air bases. Canada also set up a hospital near the battle lines to care for wounded soldiers.

A ceasefire was negotiated on March 3, 1991, and the Gulf War officially ended. No Canadians were killed during the fighting. Canadian troops remained near the Iraq-Kuwait border as peacekeepers for about two years. They monitored the zone, investigated ceasefire violations and cleared land mines.

PROFILE

Nellie Cournoyea

Nellie Cournoyea grew up in the traditional way of her people, the Inuvialuit of the Mackenzie Delta. Her family travelled and hunted on the Beaufort Sea shore. By the time she was eight, Nellie was interested in politics and had the job of recording what was said at community meetings.

Nellie was elected to the Northwest Territories legislature in 1979, and then

elected as premier in 1991 — becoming the first female Inuk in this position in Canada.

Stepping down as premier in 1995, Nellie became head of the company that manages the lands and money she helped negotiate in a 1984 land claim. She continues to work hard to help her people determine their own future.

1992 Blue Jays win the World Series

Canada cheered on October 24, 1992, when the Toronto Blue Jays became the first Canadian baseball team to win the World Series. The Blue Jays play in the American League and had only played their first game in 1977. No

team in the league had ever won the championship in so few years.

The Blue Jays won the World Series again in 1993 after Joe Carter's winning home run. They were the first team in almost 20 years to win two years in a row!

The team has also set many spectator attendance records. More than six million fans came out to watch them play in their first four seasons, and in 1993 alone, more than four million fans attended their home games.

1993 First female prime minister

As a teenager, Kim Campbell dared to think that one day she would become prime minister. She tested her political wings in high school. No girl at her school had ever been elected student council president, but Kim ran and won. And at university, she became the first female president of her first-year class.

Kim's election as a Member of Parliament (MP) for the Conservative Party in 1988 was a close call. She won by fewer than 300 votes. Although most new MPs usually wait a few years before getting Cabinet posts, Prime Minister Brian Mulroney made Kim minister of Indian affairs right away. The next year, he gave her the job of minister of justice, and in 1993, she became minister of national defence and veterans affairs.

Kim did well, but by the early 1990s, Brian Mulroney was very unpopular and so was his party. When he resigned as leader of the Conservative Party in 1993, Kim quickly entered the race to replace him. She won and took over as prime minster.

But Kim's triumph was short-lived because it was soon time for another federal election. In her campaign, she promised a "new way of doing politics," but voters didn't care. They just wanted to get rid of the Conservatives. Only two Conservatives were elected in 1993, and Kim wasn't one of them.

1994 Parti Québécois in power

Since the Charlottetown Accord's failure in 1992 (page 76), the separatist movement in Quebec had grown stronger. A year earlier, a new federal political party was formed — the Bloc Québécois. It would become known as a separatist party in Parliament.

The Parti Québécois (page 67), a separatist party on the provincial level, came into power in Quebec in 1994. Its leader, Jacques Parizeau, became premier of Quebec. In a referendum the following year, the party gained almost enough votes — 49.42 percent — to allow Quebec to begin the process of separating from Canada.

Separatists were inspired by the fiery speeches of Lucien Bouchard, leader and founder of the Bloc Québécois. He would become premier of Quebec from 1996 to 2001. The 1995 referendum had the largest voter turnout in Quebec history.

1995 Craig Kielburger founds Kids Can Free the Children

On the morning of April 19, 1995, while searching for the comics in the daily newspaper, 12-year-old Craig Kielburger was stunned by a photo of a child labourer his age from Pakistan who had battled bad working conditions and been murdered for his protests. It made Craig wonder about kids' working conditions around the world, and child poverty, health and safety.

That year, Craig and his brother, Marc, founded Kids Can Free the Children (later, Free the Children). It has since become the world's largest network of kids helping kids and has affected millions of children in more than 45 countries.

Travelling around the world, talking with young people and meeting with political leaders are just some of Craig's many activities. "Young people have a great deal to contribute," says Craig. "We may not have all the answers, but we are willing to learn — there is no shortage of energy and enthusiasm." For his work, Craig was nominated for the Nobel Peace Prize.

1996 Alanis Morissette tops the charts

Alanis Morissette is an alt-rock singer-songwriter who has won many top music awards in Canada and the United States. Her breakthrough album, *Jagged Little Pill*, was released in 1995. It stayed at the top of the charts for 19 straight weeks in 1996. The album would go on to sell 33 million copies worldwide and become the second-bestselling album by a female musician (after another Canadian, Shania Twain!).

Alanis has since recorded many more albums and has acted in plays, television shows and movies. She is also known for her activism and has helped raise awareness around environmental issues and eating disorders.

1997 Lilith Fair

Sarah McLachlan describes her young self as having been "your typical teenage rebel with a skateboard and a bad attitude." Although she began her music career studying classical guitar, piano and voice, she soon changed to pop. Today, she's a talented singer and songwriter, known for her very personal lyrics, beautiful melodies and high, sweet voice.

Helping other women in music is very important to Sarah. From 1997 to 1999, she organized Lilith Fair as an all-female music festival. In 1997, it was the most successful North American concert tour and sold more than 22 million albums. It also raised more than $7 million for charities.

One of the many charities that Sarah supports is the Sarah McLachlan School of Music, which gives free music classes to at-risk youth in Vancouver.

"As a kid," she says, "music saved my life; having that one thing that I knew I was good at made all the difference."

Did You Know?

In 1997, the Confederation Bridge was completed to connect Prince Edward Island to New Brunswick. Before then, people on the island had to travel by ferry to get to the mainland.

1998 Nisga'a Treaty

After 25 years of negotiation, the Nisga'a Treaty was settled in 1998. The treaty granted the Nisga'a people of British Columbia ownership of some of their ancient lands in the northwest of the province. It stated they could elect their own government, which could make its own laws. The laws would affect everyone on Nisga'a territory, but they had to fit with other Canadian laws.

The Nisga'a treaty was signed by Nisga'a leaders and representatives of Queen Elizabeth in 1999. It serves as a model as other Aboriginal peoples seek settlement of long-standing land claims.

1999 Nunavut

In 1999, the Inuit got something they had been striving for since the 1970s — the eastern portion of the Northwest Territories became a separate territory called Nunavut. Iqaluit was named the territory's capital. The name Nunavut means "our land" in Inuktitut, one of the main languages spoken by the Inuit. The new territory's flag includes an inukshuk (below), one of the stone landmarks built by Inuit people. About 85 percent of Nunavut's people are Inuit. Paul Okalik became the first premier.

As a territory, Nunavut doesn't have the same self-governing powers as a province. But it is run largely by the Inuit, who hold senior positions in the public service as well as in government.

Declaration of Kinship and Cooperation

The Assembly of First Nations represents Aboriginal peoples in Canada. At a meeting on the land of the Coast Salish people in Vancouver in the summer of 1999, the Assembly of First Nations met with its American equivalent, the National Congress of American Indians, to sign the Declaration of Kinship and Cooperation. This declaration states:

We, the people, knowing that the Creator placed us here on Mother Earth as sovereign nations, and seeking to live in peace, freedom and prosperity with all humanity in accordance with our own traditional laws, are united in our sacred relationship with the land, air, water and resources of our ancestral territories. We are bound by common origin and history, aspiration and experience, and we are brothers and sisters, leaders and warriors of our nations …

A NEW MILLENNIUM 2000–2017

Many Canadians and people around the world anticipated the new millennium nervously. They were afraid computers wouldn't be able to distinguish between the years 1900 and 2000 since computers often only looked at the last two digits to determine the year. Some people believed that this could cause devastating mechanical failures, such as extensive power outages. The situation became known as the Millennium Bug or the Y2K problem. ("Y" stands for "year," and "2K" stands for "2000.") Luckily it caused very few difficulties.

In the new millennium, Canadians depended more and more on technology. The internet and smartphones changed the way people accessed information and communicated.

The millennium's first decade included two worldwide economic crises, but Canada recovered more quickly than many countries. In the years leading up to 2017, Canadians looked forward to their country's 150th birthday with excitement and pride.

2000 Margaret Atwood's Booker Prize

Margaret Atwood is one of Canada's most well-known and versatile writers. She has written novels, short stories and poems, as well as books for kids. Her work has been adapted into plays, TV shows, movies and even an opera.

Margaret published her first book, a volume of poetry, in 1961. Five years later, when she was just 27, her second book of poetry, *The Circle Game*, won the Governor General's Literary Award. Margaret began writing novels in 1969, and 16 years later she won a second Governor General's Award for her book *The Handmaid's Tale*.

In 2000, she won the Booker-McConnell Prize (now called the Man Booker Prize for Fiction) — an important book award in Britain — for her novel *The Blind Assassin*. Her writing has been translated into more than 40 languages.

Human rights are important to Margaret, and she has worked for many years with Amnesty International, which strives to free people who have been unjustly imprisoned because of their beliefs. Fighting censorship of writers is a priority for her, too.

Margaret is also an inventor. She created the LongPen, which uses video and robotics to allow an author to sign a book from a distance. As well, in 2014, Margaret became the first of 100 writers to take part in the Future Library project. Her story will not be printed or read until 2114!

Did You Know?

Michael Ondaatje was the first Canadian to win the Booker-McConnell Prize. He won in 1992 for his novel *The English Patient*.

2001 Afghanistan War

Canada sent soldiers to Afghanistan in southwestern Asia in October 2001 after terrorists attacked the United States on September 11 of that year. Afghanistan was sheltering the terrorists. Thousands of Canadians joined soldiers from other countries heading overseas to make sure another terrorist attack wouldn't happen again.

Canadian soldiers worked hard to stop the terrorists, establish peace and help reconstruct roads, schools and more. Then in 2006, Canadian artillery, soldiers and tanks were sent to the very dangerous Kandahar province in southern Afghanistan to fight the terrorists.

After five years of fighting and several major battles, Canada ended its combat role

in Afghanistan in 2011. Some Canadian soldiers stayed to train the Afghanistan police force and army and to continue helping the country rebuild. The last Canadian soldiers left Afghanistan in 2014.

More than 40 000 Canadians served in Afghanistan. In total, 158 Canadians were killed and more than 600 were wounded in the struggle to bring peace and security to the country.

2002 Africville commemorated

On July 5, 2002, a plaque was unveiled in Halifax, Nova Scotia, commemorating the national historic importance of Africville. This was an area in the city's outskirts that was first settled by freed black slaves from the United States in the mid-1800s. Africville grew as black people from other communities moved there.

The people of Africville faced discrimination and isolation in their community. Africville never had electricity, running water, proper roads or street lights. Many residents had health problems because of the poor conditions.

Starting in 1964, the people of Africville were relocated so a bridge and highway could be built there. Their homes — and their church, which was a hub of the community — were demolished.

Africvillians wanted the government to recognize that their community had been treated unfairly and that their town was an important place in Canadian history. In 1996, Africville was finally declared a national historic site. On February 24, 2010, the mayor of Halifax apologized to the people of Africville. The following year, the church that had meant so much to the community was reopened after being rebuilt.

2003 Same-sex marriage

Canada took a big step towards equal rights on June 10, 2003, when same-sex marriage in Ontario became legal. The province was the third place in the world and the first in North America to legalize marriage between two men or two women. Then in 2005, the Canadian government legalized same-sex marriage across the whole country.

Michael Leshner and Michael Stark were Canada's first legally married same-sex couple. They feel their wedding stands for equality, hope and inclusion.

2004 Chantal Petitclerc wins gold

As a young child, Chantal Petitclerc of Quebec wasn't athletic. But when she was 13, an accident left her paralyzed from the waist down, and she decided to get involved in sports to stay in shape. A track coach noticed her determination and suggested she try wheelchair racing. She soon won medals at the Paralympic Games, including five gold medals in 2004.

In addition to training, Chantal has also worked as a television host and a sports commentator on the radio. "I'm good at my job," she says, "and it just so happens that I'm also in a wheelchair." Chantal also campaigns hard to have wheelchair racing recognized as an official sport at the Olympic Games.

"Happiness is like a medal. It's won by how you live every day."

— Chantal Petitclerc

2005 Steve Nash, MVP

One of the greatest point guards of all time, Steve Nash became the first Canadian to receive the National Basketball Association's (NBA's) Most Valuable Player Award in 2005. He received the award again the following year. Steve was a good player because he was skilled at handling the ball, making plays and shooting. He was also very good at anticipating where the ball would go next. His teammates liked playing with him, and he worked very hard.

Steve also helps many charities. In 2006, *Time* magazine named him one of the 100 most influential people in the world. At the 2010 Winter Olympics in Vancouver, Steve became the first NBA player to carry the Olympic torch.

"I believe the measure of a person's life is the effect they have on others."

— Steve Nash

2006 Toronto FC

Torontonians found out on May 11, 2006, that there would be a new team in town. Toronto FC was the first Major League Soccer team in Canada. FC stands for "Football Club" — soccer is called football in many parts of the world.

The team began playing in April 2007. Fans loved them so much that the first three seasons sold out. Now, Toronto FC plays against teams from Edmonton, Montreal, Ottawa and Vancouver in the Amway Canadian Championship. The team has won four consecutive times from 2009 to 2012.

Toronto FC plays at BMO (short for Bank of Montreal) Field. It's the largest stadium in Canada specifically built for soccer.

2007 Debate over the Arctic

Who owns the Arctic lands and waters above Canada? In 2007, this question was debated by the five countries that border on the Arctic Ocean: Canada, Denmark, Norway, Russia and the United States. Canada claims the territory, largely because the Inuit have lived there for thousands of years. But other countries say the waterways are international.

As the climate changes, the North's ice is melting. That means more ships can travel through the open water for military reasons, to transport goods and to carry tourists. There is also more access to its natural resources, such as fish, minerals, oil, water and more.

In July 2007, Prime Minister Stephen Harper announced that Canada was developing a port on the Arctic Ocean and purchasing a fleet of Arctic patrol ships. The debate heated up the following month when two mini-submarines planted a Russian flag on the ocean floor at the North Pole, claiming the area for Russia.

As the climate continues to change, along with technology to extract natural resources, the question of who owns the Arctic will become more important.

2008 Residential schools apology

Around the time of Confederation in 1867, there was a strong push to make Aboriginal people more like other Canadians. The government wanted Aboriginal people to abandon their past, their customs and their languages. Starting in the 1880s, this push for assimilation took its saddest turn yet. Children as young as six years old were taken from their families and placed in the "care" of strangers at residential schools.

When the children arrived at a residential school, their long hair was cut off, their names were changed to more "Canadian-sounding" names and they were punished or beaten if they spoke their own language. Many suffered mental, physical and sexual abuse from school authorities. They were seldom permitted to visit their parents. The parents and relatives were allowed to visit only for very short times, if at all.

For many years, children in residential schools often went hungry and spent the majority of

their time doing menial chores. The little education they received at the school didn't prepare them to find jobs. And they were also robbed of the chance to learn traditional hunting and fishing skills. Thousands of children never returned home but died mysteriously at the schools. Many of those who did return were damaged, and others had a hard time fitting into their traditional cultures.

Most residential schools were closed by the mid-1970s. The last residential school, located in Saskatchewan, was closed in 1996. The Truth and Reconciliation Commission of Canada was established on June 2, 2008, to gather information about residential school abuse and propose action. On December 15, 2015, the Commission released its final report, and its documents are now housed at the National Centre for Truth and Reconciliation in Winnipeg. On June 11, 2008, the prime minister issued an apology to the survivors of the residential schools.

2009 BlackBerry's smartphone

In 2009, more than one-fifth of all the smartphones used around the world were made by a Canadian company called BlackBerry. Based in Waterloo, Ontario, the company was originally called Research In Motion (RIM) but was renamed BlackBerry in 2013.

The company's first device was an email pager released in 1999, and it was one of the first to let people check their email from the palm of their hands. In 2003, the BlackBerry smartphone was made available. The device got its name because the buttons on its keyboard look like the little "balls" on a blackberry. It allowed users to email, phone, text and browse the web.

2010 Frank Gehry's buildings

Many of Frank Gehry's buildings are already world-famous tourist attractions. So it's no wonder that in 2010 he was named the most important architect of our time.

His Guggenheim Museum in Bilbao, Spain, is thought by many to have changed the world of architecture. Made of glass, limestone and titanium, the museum's sweeping curves are daring and spectacular.

In Canada, Frank is best known for his renovation of the Art Gallery of Ontario in Toronto (right). As a child, he had lived in that area. Frank created a bold spiral staircase for the museum, as well as a wood-and-glass gallery that has been described as a "crystal ship drifting through the city."

Using computers and other technology, Frank continues to push the limits. His designs are bold and unusual but can still be warm and inviting. He takes inspiration from many sources, but especially from fish and the way they move.

2011 Jack Layton and the NDP

For the first time in Canada's history, on May 2, 2011, the New Democratic Party (NDP) (page 64) became Canada's Official Opposition. That meant that in the federal election, the NDP won the second-highest number of seats in Canada's House of Commons. The party elected 103 Members of Parliament, which was an NDP record. That election also set a record for NDP votes in Quebec.

Jack Layton was the leader of the NDP for its historic win. This social activist was well known for fighting climate change, homelessness, violence against women and many other important issues. Jack was able to assist groups within his party agree when they had very different views. In Parliament, people were also impressed by how he helped the various parties work together.

"Love is better than anger. Hope is better than fear. Optimism is better than despair. So let us be loving, hopeful and optimistic. And we'll change the world."

— Jack Layton

Soon after the election, Jack announced he had cancer. He had battled the disease before, so people were hopeful he'd be successful again. But sadly, Jack died on August 22, 2011. A few days earlier, he wrote a letter that was to be read after he died. He encouraged other cancer sufferers to keep fighting and noted how inspired he had always been by young Canadians.

2012 Idle No More

In November 2012, many Aboriginal people were angry about laws and policy changes that the Canadian government was planning to make. They were especially unhappy about the government's Bill C-45. Aboriginal groups across the country felt the bill would not only reduce their authority and rights, but would also hurt the environment for all Canadians.

Three Aboriginal women and one non-Aboriginal woman all from Saskatchewan began emailing each other about Bill C-45. That led them to set up a Facebook page, which they named "Idle No More." The name means they felt Aboriginal peoples needed to stop waiting for someone else to tell the government how they felt — it was time to take action.

First Nations, Métis, Inuit and non-Aboriginal people soon all got involved. Idle No More supporters held protests, rallies and educational sessions they called teach-ins. In shopping malls, flash mobs took part in round dances. Theresa Spence, chief of the Attawapiskat First Nation, declared a hunger strike in December 2012 to focus attention on Aboriginal issues.

In early 2013, a group of just seven left a James Bay Cree community to journey 1600 km (1000 mi.) to Ottawa. By the time they arrived, their number had grown to about 400 trekkers.

One reason Idle No More spread so quickly was because it was a grassroots movement, which means it was organized by ordinary people. Their actions made people across Canada and around the world think about Aboriginal rights.

Aboriginal people continue to want new government processes for dealing with Aboriginal land claims, as well as to be fully recognized as the first people living in Canada. As well, rather than just settling land claims, they want new principles that focus on reconciliation.

2013 Alice Munro's Nobel Prize

Canada's most famous short-story author, Alice Munro, started writing stories when she was a teenager. At first, she wrote adventure stories — often with herself as the hero. She began by writing in the style of other writers, but gradually developed her own distinctive voice.

Alice writes about ordinary people and situations, painting intense word-pictures of how people think and behave. Many of her stories look at the lives of women, from teenage girls to middle-aged women and seniors. She describes her writing as "autobiographical in form, but not in fact."

Very skilled at writing dialogue, Alice is also extremely insightful and observant. Because of this, she can create such realistic characters that it's easy for readers to see themselves in her stories.

A lot of care goes into Alice's work — she often writes and re-writes over and over, making small but important changes. All of this effort has paid off: Alice has won many prizes around the world for her writing, including winning the Governor General's Literary Award several times. In 2013, she won the Nobel Prize for Literature — the richest literary prize in the world.

2014 Franklin's lost ship

For almost 170 years, explorers and scientists had been searching the cold arctic waters off the north coast of Canada for traces of an expedition led by British explorer John Franklin. This experienced captain, his crew and two ships — the HMS *Erebus* and the HMS *Terror* — had set sail from England in 1845, but never returned after getting trapped in the ice. Their journey would famously become known as the Franklin Expedition.

For years, only a few traces of the expedition were found, even though many groups searched for Franklin and his ships. In the 1980s, Canadian anthropologist Owen Beattie examined bodies of the crew that had been buried in graves on Beechey Island, Nunavut. He determined the crew had suffered from lead poisoning, likely caused by poor seals on the tins of food they had eaten. But the final resting place of Franklin and of his ships was still a mystery.

Historians knew the Franklin Expedition had journeyed at least as far as Hat Island. Using the information provided by the Inuit, as well as modern technology, scientists from various Canadian organizations finally found the *Erebus* in September 2014. Divers recovered a brass bell from the ship and also found cannons, pulley blocks and ropes.

2015 Year of Sport

When cities across the country hosted games in the FIFA (Fédération Internationale de Football Association) Women's World Cup in 2015, it was the first time Canada hosted the tournament. This was just one of the many championships held in the country that year. No wonder Governor General David Johnston declared 2015 the "Year of Sport."

The World Junior Ice Hockey Championship took place in Toronto and Montreal in January. The next month, the Canada Winter Games were held in Prince George, British Columbia. In March, Halifax hosted the Ford World Men's Curling Championship. Toronto was home to the Pan American Games in July, followed by the Parapan American Games.

A New Cabinet

Liberal Party leader Justin Trudeau was elected prime minister in October 2015. A few weeks later, he announced which Members of Parliament would work closely with him as ministers in his Cabinet.

Justin's Cabinet included immigrants, Aboriginal people, religious minorities, a quadriplegic person and even former astronaut Marc Garneau (page 74).

For the first time in Canadian history, the Cabinet had an equal number of men and women. When asked why this was important, Justin replied, "Because it's 2015."

2016 World Festival of Children's Theatre

Stratford, Ontario, hosted the World Festival of Children's Theatre in June 2016. This was the first time the festival was held in North America and the theme was "My World, Our Planet." About 500 kids from 20 countries performed plays about what was important to them and how they saw the world.

Stratford was chosen to host the festival because it's home to the Stratford Festival. This world-famous celebration of theatre focuses on plays by British writer William Shakespeare but also presents ancient Greek plays, musicals and more. The Stratford Festival was one of the first arts festivals in Canada.

2017 Canada turns 150!

Every year on July 1, Canadians celebrate their country's birthday with parades, fireworks, picnics, parties and much more. And 2017 marked a very special birthday — Canada's 150th!

An important birthday is a good time to look back at the incredible Canadians and events that have made the country great. It's also a time to think about what Canada means to you. For instance, many Canadians are especially proud of the country's diversity. Canada has a wide variety of customs, landscapes, peoples, foods and sports!

Canada is also a strong, peaceful country, full of people who treat each other with respect. Aboriginal peoples can trace their ancestry back to the first people to live here. And other Canadians are descended from immigrants. Because of this diversity, Canadians are known for working together to create a country that is "the True North strong and free." The achievements and innovations of brave Canadians have given the country a rich past and a promising future.

Welcome to Canada

Many communities across Canada hold citizenship ceremonies on July 1 each year. To become a Canadian citizen, immigrants must first answer questions about such subjects as Canada's history, economy and government. People wanting to become Canadians may be asked how Members of Parliament are chosen (they're elected), what the word *Inuit* means ("the people") or the name of the capital of their province or territory.

At a citizenship ceremony, new Canadians take the Oath of Citizenship, in which each person promises to be faithful to Queen Elizabeth and to observe the laws of Canada and fulfill his or her duties as a Canadian citizen. They then receive a citizenship certificate. After speeches by special guests, everyone sings the national anthem.

GREAT CANADIANS

Many strong, brave and determined people have made Canada a great country since 1867. Some have changed Canada and even transformed the world. There are too many to mention in one book, but here are a few more great Canadians who have made their nation proud.

Max Aitken, Lord Beaverbrook (1879–1964) was a wealthy Canadian businessperson, British politician and newspaper owner. During World War I, he sent reports on Canadian troops back to Canada from Europe. For his work in the war and in politics, Max was named 1st Baron Beaverbrook.

Louise Arbour (1947–) is known internationally as a fighter for human rights. She served as the United Nations high commissioner for human rights, the first Canadian to have this responsibility. Her role was to give a voice to victims around the world whose rights have been abused.

Pitseolak Ashoona (1904–1983) was one of Canada's best-known Inuit artists. She created more than 7000 drawings and 250 prints over her career. Her art's imagery and style recall traditional Inuit life. The energy and humour she put into her work makes it both popular and timeless.

William "Billy" Bishop (1894–1956) was a fighter pilot during World War I who took part in 170 air battles during the war. He earned the Distinguished Flying Cross after scoring 25 victories in just 12 days. He was also awarded the Victoria Cross, the highest of all British honours for bravery in battle.

Henri Bourassa (1868–1952) founded Montreal's *Le Devoir*, one of Canada's most important newspapers. He was also a politician and champion of French language rights and culture in Canada, and felt Canada should be more independent from Britain.

Rosemary Brown (1930–2003) was the first black woman elected to British Columbia's provincial legislature. Two years later, the New Democratic Party asked Rosemary to run for the party's leadership. Even though she lost, she raised awareness of women's and black people's rights.

Floyd Chalmers (1898–1993) was a successful businessperson and magazine publisher. He donated money to many causes, including forming the Canadian Opera Company and building a theatre for the Stratford Festival in Stratford, Ontario. The Chalmers Program still helps artists today.

Don Cherry (1934–) is Canada's most famous hockey commentator. He's well known for speaking his mind, being patriotic — and for his flashy, colourful suits and his bull terrier Blue. Once a professional hockey player and coach, Don prefers players who have a tough, physical style.

Adrienne Clarkson (1939–) was Canada's Governor General from 1999 to 2005. She was the first person from a visible minority to hold this position. Her family came to Canada in 1942 as refugees from Hong Kong. Adrienne worked as a broadcaster for the Canadian Broadcasting Corporation, as well as a journalist.

Leonard Cohen (1934–) was known for his poetry before he became a singer and songwriter. His trademark low, raspy monotone and poetic lyrics have made him famous around the world, and artists from many countries have recorded his melancholy songs.

Stompin' Tom Connors (1936–2013) wrote more than 500 songs, and many have become part of Canadian culture. Titles such as "Bud the Spud," "The Hockey Song" and "Sudbury Saturday Night" are some of his best known. Stompin' Tom received his nickname because he stomped as he sang. He went on to become one of Canada's most beloved musicians.

Arthur Currie (1875–1933) was the first Canadian-born commander of the Canadian Corps. One of the most capable generals in World War I, he was known for emphasizing planning and preparation. He planned the famous Hundred Days offensive (page 37), which helped bring about the defeat of the Germans and the end of the war.

Roméo Dallaire (1946–) was head of a United Nations Peacekeeping Force in Rwanda (in Central Africa). In 1994, he worked desperately to prevent a horrible massacre there, but didn't have enough peacekeepers to stop it. Today, he continues to speak out about what happened in Rwanda and helps children who are affected by war, especially child soldiers.

Atom Egoyan (1960–) is one of Canada's most famous filmmakers. Born in Egypt, he was named Atom in honour of that country's first nuclear reactor. He has won many awards at film festivals around the world. Atom's most famous films include *The Sweet Hereafter*, *Ararat* and *Adoration*. He has also directed operas for the Canadian Opera Company.

Arthur Erickson (1924–2009) was a Vancouver architect who designed impressive buildings in Canada and around the world, including Simon Fraser University in Burnaby, British Columbia. He preferred simple materials, such as concrete, and used them to create dramatic structures.

Nancy Greene (1943–) was a downhill skier whose aggressive style earned her the nickname "Tiger." She began racing seriously at age 14, and two years later, she was fast enough to make the Olympic team. Although she didn't win that year, she would eventually win many medals — including Olympic gold — after years of hard work.

Chris Hadfield (1959–) is an astronaut who was the first Canadian to use the Canadarm (page 73), to walk in space and to command the International Space Station (ISS). He also created the first music video shot in space when he sang David Bowie's "Space Oddity" from the ISS. Using photos, tweets and videos, he greatly increased people's understanding of space.

Clara Hughes (1972–) is the only athlete to have won multiple medals at both the Winter and Summer Olympics. This cyclist and speed skater has earned six medals — only speed skater Cindy Klassen has won as many Olympic medals for Canada. Having experienced depression, Clara now speaks out about it to help others.

Michaëlle Jean (1957–) became Canada's Governor General in 2005, the first black Canadian appointed to this post. A refugee from Haiti, Michaëlle worked as a broadcaster and journalist. In 2014, she became the first female secretary-general of the Organisation internationale de la Francophonie, a group representing regions where French is the main language.

Pauline Johnson (1861–1913) was one of Canada's most popular writers and entertainers of her time. Part Mohawk, she was also known as Tekahionwake, which means "double life." Pauline toured all over North America and Britain, performing her poetry and speaking passionately about Canada and Aboriginal rights.

Lynn Johnston (1947–) is the cartoonist behind the comic strip "For Better or For Worse." It appears in more than 2000 newspapers in 20 countries. Lynn has won many awards for her work. As well, she's the first cartoonist to include a gay character in a popular Canadian comic strip.

Cornelius Krieghoff (1815–1872) was a famous artist who became known for his paintings of habitants (settlers in Quebec) and Aboriginal people. His pictures told interesting stories, and he knew which details to include to capture the richness — and harshness — of people's lives in Quebec at that time.

Silken Laumann (1964–) was only 19 when she won Olympic bronze in 1984 for rowing. By 1991, she was the world's top women's rower. Shortly before the 1992 Olympics, Silken was badly injured in a rowing accident. She still competed and went on to win a bronze medal.

Stephen Leacock (1869–1944) was a professor, humour writer and one of the first Canadian writers to become world-famous. The Stephen Leacock Medal for Humour is awarded every year in his honour for the funniest book written by a Canadian.

Stephen Lewis (1937–) is a politician, diplomat and author who has served as Canada's ambassador to the United Nations. Today, he's famous for fighting HIV/AIDS, especially in Africa, with his organizations AIDS-Free World and the Stephen Lewis Foundation, and standing up for women's rights.

Ashley MacIsaac (1975–) is a skilled fiddler and energetic performer. He grew up on Cape Breton Island, Nova Scotia, playing traditional Celtic music. But then, Ashley added modern dance rhythms and a punk rock edge, and his music became incredibly popular around the world.

Hart Massey (1823–1896) was a savvy businessperson who understood the importance of producing up-to-date machines. Under his leadership, his family's manufacturing company became the first in North America to export farm machinery to countries around the world. Hart gave generously to many charities and built Massey Hall in Toronto.

Joni Mitchell (1943–) is one of Canada's best-known singers and songwriters. She has written some of pop's most famous songs. Joni has won awards around the world for her unique guitar style, interesting song lyrics and light, high voice.

W. O. Mitchell (1914–1998) was an author from Weyburn, Saskatchewan, famous for his novels about prairie life, including *Who Has Seen the Wind*. He later became well known for his collection of short stories *Jake and the Kid*, which was adapted for radio and television.

Norval Morrisseau

(1932–2007) was a famous Ojibwe painter known for developing the Woodlands style of art, also known as X-ray art, used by many Aboriginal artists. His brightly coloured, high-energy paintings hang in museums and galleries around the world.

Bobby Orr (1948–) was a fast-skating defenceman who revolutionized the position with his playmaking. He is the only defenceman to win the National Hockey League (NHL) scoring title — and he did it twice. Bobby was named the NHL's best defenceman a record eight times and is one of the greatest hockey players of all time.

Grey Owl (1888–1938) became famous in North America and Britain for his love of nature and animals. He wrote books and gave speeches on the need to preserve the environment. People believed he was an Aboriginal person, but after he died, it was discovered he was actually an Englishman named Archibald Belaney. He is still admired for his work as a conservationist.

Sarah Polley (1979–) is an actor and director who makes movies that are important to society. She became an international hit as Sara Stanley in the television series *Road to Avonlea,* based on stories by Lucy Maud Montgomery (page 30). She has won many awards and was nominated for an Academy Award for Best Adapted Screenplay.

Mordecai Richler (1931–2001)

won many awards for the books he wrote for both adults and kids. His popular children's book *Jacob Two-Two Meets the Hooded Fang* was made into a movie. One of Canada's most important fiction writers, he was especially known for his humorous and witty writing about life in the Jewish neighbourhoods of Montreal.

Joseph "Joey" Smallwood

(1900–1991) was the main force behind Newfoundland joining Canada in 1949. He became the province's first premier that year and held the job for many years. Joey had a strong personality and worked to modernize education and transportation in Newfoundland.

Hayley Wickenheiser (1978–) is thought by many to be the world's greatest female hockey player. She's earned four Olympic gold medals — no Canadian has won more Olympic gold medals. In 2003, while playing on a Finnish team, she became the first woman to score in a men's pro league.

Joyce Wieland (1931–1998) was the first living female artist to be the focus of a major exhibition at the National Gallery of Canada in Ottawa. Her witty, imaginative art included paintings, drawings, collage, film, cartoons, knitting, quilting — even cake! Joyce was inspired by politics — especially women's issues — and her country.

Florence Wyle (1881–1968) and **Frances Loring** (1887–1968) showed people that sculpture is as important as other art forms. Florence is known for her sculptures of children and animals. She was the first woman sculptor given a full membership in the Royal Canadian Academy of Arts. Frances became known for her war memorials and founded the Sculptors' Society of Canada.

Index